THE SHAPE OF THE JOURNEY

Jim Harrison

JIM HARRISON

The Shape
of the Journey

NEW AND COLLECTED POEMS

COPPER CANYON PRESS

I would especially like to thank Joseph Bednarik
for his efforts and advice on this book. — J.H.

◆◆◆

Copper Canyon Press gratefully acknowledges and thanks Russell Chatham
for the use of his painting, *Sunset at Deep Creek,* oil, 30" × 24", 1994.

Printed in the United States of America.

The publication of this book was supported by grants from the Lannan Foundation,
the National Endowment for the Arts, and the Washington State Arts Commission.
Additional support was received from Marvin and Dorothy Bell, Janet and Leslie Cox,
Elliott Bay Book Company, Mimi Gardner Gates, Sammy and Bill Greenwood,
Cynthia Hartwig, Bruce S. Kahn, Carolyn Kizer, Peter Lewis/Campagne,
William Merchant and Alice Pease, James B. Swinerton, Jim and
Mary Lou Wickwire, and the many members who joined the Friends
of Copper Canyon Press campaign. Copper Canyon Press is in
residence with Centrum at Fort Worden State Park.

LIBRARY OF CONGRESS CATALOGING-IN-PUBLICATION DATA

Harrison, Jim, 1937-
The shape of the journey: new and collected poems / by Jim Harrison.
p. cm.
Includes indexes.
ISBN 1-55659-095-4
ISBN 1-55659-096-2 (deluxe limited edition)
1. Title.
PS3558.A67 S53 1998
811'.54 — DDC21
98-25501
CIP

9 8 7 6 5 4 3 2
FIRST EDITION

COPPER CANYON PRESS
Post Office Box 271
Port Townsend, Washington 98368

•••

To Lawrence Sullivan

•••

CONTENTS

•••

LOCATIONS (1968)

•••

AFTER IKKYŪ & OTHER POEMS (1996)

•••

THE SHAPE OF THE JOURNEY

Jim Harrison

INTRODUCTION

It is a laborious and brain-peeling process to edit one's collected poems. You drift and jerk back and forth between wanting to keep it all intact, and the possibility of pitching out the whole work in favor of a fresh start.

But then there are no fresh starts at age sixty and this book is the portion of my life that means the most to me. I've written a goodly number of novels and novellas but they sometimes strike me as extra, burly flesh on the true bones of my life though a few of them approach some of the conditions of poetry. There is the additional, often shattering notion gotten from reading a great deal in anthropology, that in poetry our motives are utterly similar to those who made cave paintings or petroglyphs, so that studying your own work of the past is to ruminate over artifacts, each one a signal, a remnant of a knot of perceptions that brings back to life who and what you were at the time, the past texture of what has to be termed as your "soul life."

I fear that somewhat improperly, humility arrived rather late in life. I don't mean self-doubt which is quite another thing. The Romantic "I" with all of its inherent stormy bombast, its fungoid elevation of the most questionable aspects of personality, its totally self-referential regard of life, has tended to disappear. I recall that Bill Monroe, the bluegrass musician, said that he didn't write songs but "discovered them in the air." If you add Wallace Stevens's contention that "technique is the proof of seriousness," we come closer to the warm, red heart of the matter. Of course you come to realize that your Romantic "I" never had much to do with your poems in the first place but was mostly a fuel tank for public postures.

Another good source of humility is the dozen or so famous poets I can enumerate whose work has apparently vaporized since I published my first book, *Plain Song,* back in 1965. It's been years since I went on one, but a reasonably well-attended reading tour can give you an unjustified sense of permanence. More desirable memories are those of picking potato bugs for a dollar a day at age ten, or living in a windowless seven-dollar-a-week room in Greenwich Village with photos of Rimbaud and Lorca taped to the wall above one's pillow. A good sidebar on impermanence at the time was the arrival, every few days at the bookstore where I worked, of the eminent anthologist Oscar Williams who would carefully check the racks to make sure his work was well-displayed. In his anthologies Oscar would add an appendix with lists of the twenty-five "Chief Poets of America," and perhaps fifty "Chief Poets of the World," featuring photos, which invariably included Oscar and his girlfriend, Gene Derwood. This added a tinge of cynicism about literary life to a nineteen-year-old. But then we have always had our Colley Cibbers, our Oscar Williamses, our Casey Kasems trying to establish an infantile worth with premature canons. By nature a poet is permanently inconsolable, but there is a balm in the idea that in geological terms we all own the same measure of immortality, though our beloved Shakespeare and a few others will live until the planet dies.

Of course any concerns over what has actually happened in American poetry in the last thirty-five years or so are inevitably fragile if you're not a scholar. There was obviously a healthy diaspora during which there were Pyrrhic wars, the exfoliation into the MFA "creative writing" period, and now apparently lapsing into a new faux-sincere Victorianism. If there is health it is in the biodiversity of the product. I suppose I was too overexposed as a graduate student in comparative literature to both the wretchedness of xenophobia and the repetitive vagaries of literary history, to maintain interest. If after a few days I can't mentally summon the essence of the work I've been reading I simply don't care who says it's good and why. The impulse to choose up sides is better abandoned in grade school. I recall how startled I was in my early twenties in Boston when I discovered I was not allowed to like Roethke, the Lowell of *Life Studies,* and also Duncan, Snyder, and Olson, the latter three whom I came to know. Not that I was above the frays, just that I was unequal to maintaining interest in them. I remember that in my brief time in academia, in our rather shabby rental in Stony Brook, we had gatherings of poets as diverse as Denise Levertov, Louis Simpson, James Wright, and Robert Duncan who all rather effortlessly got along. But then, the poem is the thing and most of the rest are variations on the theme of gossip.

If I attempt to slip rather lightly over my own volumes, distinctly visual images arise with each book, emerging from what job I had at the time to support my family, what studio or kitchen table I used to write the work, where we lived at the time, and my usual obsession with what kind of cheap wine I was drinking. Other images include what dog or dogs were our beloved companions, and what cats tormented or loved the dogs. This is what I meant by cave paintings or petroglyphs: cooking our lives down we don't really cook away our Pleistocene ingredients. I am reminded that in the splendid history of Icelandic culture everyone is expected to at least try to turn a hand to poetry. I am also reminded of Heidegger's contention that poetry is not elevated common language but that common language is reduced, banalized poetry.

1. *Plain Song.* My first book, published through the efforts of Denise Levertov, who had become a consulting editor at W.W. Norton. Nothing equals, of course, the first book, which is at the very least a tenuous justification of what you insisted was your calling. I had been eating the contents of world poetry since I was fifteen and without any idea of what to spit out. I collected *Botteghe Oscure,* but also Bly's magazines *The Fifties* and *The Sixties.* I was obsessed with Lorca, W.C. Williams, Apollinaire, Rimbaud, and Walt Whitman but none of it much shows in the book, which is mostly poems out of my rural past. It was primarily written in Boston where I was a road man for a book wholesaler; but I had my first real exposure to other poets, most of whom hung out in Gordon Cairnie's Grolier Book Shop, in Cambridge. I also spent some time with Charles Olson in Gloucester but was too bent on my own obsessions to digest any of his gospel.

2. *Locations.* Quite a different book. I couldn't endure the city so we moved back to rural northern Michigan, where I worked as a common

construction laborer and studied Pound and Rilke at night, also T'ang Dynasty poets. Rilke can be viewed as some sort of ornate European shaman who devours his imperiled readers who must wonder if they are ever going to emerge. I was also drawn to Stravinsky at the time, whom I endlessly played on our thirty-dollar record player in the living room of our thirty-dollar-a-month house that never got warm. I think this fascination with classical music lead me to the "suite" form.

3. *Outlyer & Ghazals*. An old professor and friend, Herbert Weisinger, engineered my getting a long-abandoned master's degree and dragged us out of northern Michigan to Stony Brook, Long Island. This was likely a good thing with an exposure to hundreds of poets and to New York City, where in my late teens I had been a solitary buffoon. I began writing ghazals as a reaction to being terribly overstuffed with culture.

4. *Letters to Yesenin*. An utterly desperate period with multiple clinical depressions. I was still in high school when I discovered a Yarmolinsky anthology of Russian poetry and became fascinated with it, aided later by the splendor of the New York Public Library. I was temperamentally unfit for academic life and we had moved back to northern Michigan, aided by two deceptive grants from the National Endowment, and the Guggenheim Foundation; "deceptive" because I did not see the day of reckoning when I'd somehow have to make a living again. I went to Russia with Dan Gerber in 1972 and followed the tracks of Yesenin, Dostoyevsky, Voznesensky and Akhmatova, poets we loved. I tried everything to make a living, including journalism and novel-writing, neither of which quite supported us. For nearly a decade we averaged ten grand a year. The *Letters to Yesenin* were an act of desperation and survival.

5. *Returning to Earth*. More from this occasionally grim period, leavened by the fact that we lived in a relatively poor area and our condition was scarcely unique. This long poem was, I suspect, both a conscious and unconscious attempt to internalize the natural world I had been so strongly drawn to after a childhood injury that had blinded my left eye.

4

6. *Selected and New Poems.* Probably premature but then I had finally had a financial success with a book of novellas, *Legends of the Fall,* and my publisher was quite willing to collect my poetry.

7. *The Theory and Practice of Rivers.* Written at a remote cabin nestled by a river in Michigan's Upper Peninsula, and at our farm in Leelanau County. It was an attempt to render what could keep one alive in a progressively more unpleasant world with some of the difficulties of my own doing in the world of script writing in New York and Hollywood. It is certainly not my *métier* but it was a well-paid option to teaching, at which I was a failure. I used to think it was virtuous to stay distant from academia but gradually I realized that any way a "serious writer" can get a living is fine. The problem with both town and gown is the temptation to write for one's peers rather than from the heart. The same is true of the multifoliate forms of regionalism.

8. *After Ikkyū.* A largely misunderstood book. Dan Wakefield has noted that in our *haute* culture books thought to have any religious content are largely ignored. I have practiced a profoundly inept sort of Zen for twenty-five years and this book is an attempt to return to the more elemental facts of life, unsuffocated by habituation, conditioning, or learning.

9. "Geo-Bestiary." The new work included in these *New and Collected Poems.* A rather wild-eyed effort to resume contact with reality after writing a long novel that had drawn me far from the world I like to call home.

— *Jim Harrison*
Grand Marais, Michigan
May 7, 1998

PLAIN SONG

to Linda

1965

POEM

Form is the woods: the beast,
a bobcat padding through red sumac,
the pheasant in brake or goldenrod
that he stalks – both rise to the flush,
the brief low flutter and catch in air;
and trees, rich green, the moving of boughs
and the separate leaf, yield
to conclusions they do not care about
or watch – the dead, frayed bird,
the beautiful plumage,
the spoor of feathers
and slight, pink bones.

SKETCH FOR A JOB-APPLICATION BLANK

My left eye is blind and jogs like
a milky sparrow in its socket;
my nose is large and never flares
in anger, the front teeth, bucked,
but not in lechery – I sucked
my thumb until the age of twelve.
O my youth was happy and I was never lonely
though my friends called me "pig eye"
and the teachers thought me loony.

> (When I bruised, my psyche kept intact:
> I fell from horses, and once a cow but never
> pigs – a neighbor lost a hand to a sow.)

But I had some fears:
the salesman of eyes,
his case was full of fishy baubles,
against black velvet, jeweled gore,
the great cocked hoof of a Belgian mare,
a nest of milk snakes by the water trough,
electric fences,
my uncle's hounds,
the pump arm of an oil well,
the chop and whir of a combine in the sun.

From my ancestors, the Swedes,
I suppose I inherit the love of rainy woods,
kegs of herring and neat whiskey –
I remember long nights of pinochle,
the bulge of Redman in my grandpa's cheek;

the rug smelled of manure and kerosene.
They laughed loudly and didn't speak for days.

    (But on the other side, from the German Mennonites,
    their rag-smoke prayers and porky daughters
    I got intolerance, and aimless diligence.)

In '51 during a revival I was saved:
I prayed on a cold register for hours
and woke up lame. I was baptized
by immersion in the tank at Williamston –
the rusty water stung my eyes.
I left off the old things of the flesh
but not for long – one night beside a pond
she dried my feet with her yellow hair.
    O actual event dead quotient
    cross become green
I still love Jubal but pity Hagar.

    (Now self is the first sacrament
    who loves not the misery and taint
    of the present tense is lost.
    I strain for a lunar arrogance.
        Light macerates
        the lamp infects
  warmth, more warmth, I cry.)

DAVID

He is young. The father is dead.
Outside, a cold November night,
the mourners' cars are parked upon the lawn;
beneath the porch light three
brothers talk to three sons
and shiver without knowing it.
His mind's all black thickets
and blood; he knows
flesh slips quietly off the bone,
he knows no last looks,
that among the profusion of flowers
the lid is closed to hide
what no one could bear –
that metal rends the flesh,
he knows beneath the white-pointed
creatures, stars,
that in the distant talk of brothers,
the father is dead.

EXERCISE

Hear this touch: grass parts
for the snake,
in furrows
soil curves around itself,
a rock topples into a lake,
roused organs,
fur against cloth,
arms unfold,
at the edge of a clearing
fire selects new wood.

A SEQUENCE OF WOMEN

I

I've known her too long:
we devour as two mirrors,
opposed,
swallow each other a thousand
times at midpoints,
lost in the black center
of the other.

II

She sits on the bed,
breasts slack,
watching a curl of dust
float through a ray of sun,
drift down to a corner.
So brief this meeting
with a strange child —
Do I want to be remembered?
Only as a mare might know
the body of her rider,
the pressure of legs
unlike any other.

III

The girl who was once my mistress
is dead now, I learn, in childbirth.
I thought that long ago women ceased
dying this way.

To set records straight, our enmity
relaxes, I wrote a verse for her —
to dole her by pieces, ring finger
and lock of hair.

But I'm a poor Midas to turn her golden,
to make a Helen, grand whore, of this graceless
girl; the sparrow that died was only
a sparrow:

Though in the dark, she doesn't sleep.
On cushions, embraced by silk, no lover
comes to her. In the first light when birds
stir she does not stir or sing. Oh eyes can't
focus to this dark.

NORTHERN MICHIGAN

On this back road the land
has the juice taken out of it:

stump fences surround nothing
worth their tearing down

by a deserted filling station
a Veedol sign, the rusted hulk

of a Frazer, "live bait"
on battered tin.

        A barn
with half a tobacco ad
owns the greenness of a manure
pile

a half-moon on a privy door
a rope swinging from an elm. A

collapsed henhouse, a pump
with the handle up

the orchard with wild tangled branches.

    ♦♦♦

In the far corner of the pasture,
in the shadow of the woodlot
a herd of twenty deer:

        three bucks

are showing off –
they jump in turn across the fence,
flanks arch and twist to get higher
in the twilight
as the last light filters
through the woods.

RETURNING AT NIGHT

Returning at night

there's a catalpa moth
in the barberry

on the table the flowers
left alone turned black

in the root cellar
the potato sprouts
creeping through the door
glisten white and tubular
in the third phase
of the moon.

FAIR/BOY CHRISTIAN TAKES A BREAK

This other speaks of bones, blood-wet
and limber, the rock in bodies. He takes
me to the slaughterhouse, where lying
sprawled, as a giant coil of rope,
the bowels of cattle. At the county fair
we pay an extra quarter to see the her-
maphrodite. We watch the secret air tube
blow up the skirts of the farm girls,
tanned to the knees then strangely white.
We eat spareribs and pickled eggs,
the horses tear the ground to pull a load
of stone; in a burning tent we see
Fantasia do her Love Dance with the
Spaniard – they glisten with sweat, their
limbs knot together while below them farm
boys twitter like birds. Then the breasts
of a huge Negress rotate to a march in
opposing directions, and everyone stamps
and cheers, the udders shine in blurring
speed. Out of the tent we pass produce
stalls, some hung with ribbons, squash
and potatoes stacked in pyramids. A buck-
toothed girl cuts her honorable-mention
cake; when she leans to get me water
from a milk pail her breasts are chaste.
Through the evening I sit in the car (the
other is gone) while my father watches
the harness race, the 4-H talent show.
I think of St. Paul's Epistles and pray
the removal of what my troubled eyes have seen.

MORNING

The mirror tastes him
breath clouds
hands pressed against glass

in yellow morning light
a jay
flutters in unaccustomed
silence
from bush to limb of elm

a cow at breakfast
pauses
her jaws lax in momentary stillness

far off a milk truck
rattles
on the section road

light low mist
floats
over the buckwheat
through the orchard

the neighbor's dogs bark
then four roosters announce
day.

KINSHIP

Great-uncle Wilhelm, Mennonite, patriarch,
eater of blood sausage, leeks,
headcheese, salt pork,
you are led into church
by that wisp you plundered for nine children.
Your brain has sugared now,
your white beard is limp,
you talk of acres of corn
where there is only snow.
Your sister, a witch, old as a stump,
says you are punished now for the unspeakable
sin that barred you from the table for seven years.
They feed you cake to hasten your death.
Your land is divided.
Curse them but don't die.

FEBRUARY SUITE

Song,
angry bush
with the thrust of your roots
deep in this icy ground,
is there a polar sun?

•••

Month of the frozen
goat —
La Roberta says cultivate
new friends,
                profit will
be yours with patience.
Not that stars are crossed
or light to be restored —
we die from want of velocity.

And you, longest of months
with your false springs,
you don't help or care about helping,
so splendidly ignorant of us.
Today icicles fell
but they will build downward again.

•••

Who has a "fate"?
This fig tree
talks
about bad weather.

♦♦♦

Here is a man drunk –
in the glass
his blurred innocence renewed.

♦♦♦

The Great Leitzel
before falling to her death
did 249 flanges on the Roman rings –
her wrist was often raw
and bloody
but she kept it hidden.

♦♦♦

He remembers Memorial Day –
the mother's hymn to Generals.
The American Legion fires blanks
out over the lassitude of the cemetery
in memory of sons who broke
like lightbulbs in a hoarse cry
of dust.

♦♦♦

Now
behind bone
in the perfect dark
the dream of animals.

♦♦♦

To remember
the soft bellies of fish
the furred animals that were part of your youth
not for their novelty
but as fellow creatures.

♦♦♦

I look at the rifles
in their rack upon the wall:
though I know the Wars
only as history
some cellar in Europe might still
owe some of its moistness to blood.

♦♦♦

With my head on the table
I write,
my arm outstretched, in another field
of richer grain.

♦♦♦

A red-haired doll stares
at me from a highchair,
her small pink limbs twisted about
her neck.
I salute the postures of women.

♦♦♦

This hammer of joy,
this is no fist
but a wonderment got by cunning.

The first thunderstorm
of March came last night
and when I awoke the snow had passed
away, the brown grass
lay matted and pubic.

Between the snow and grass,
somewhere into the ground with the rain
a long year has gone.

TRAVERSE CITY ZOO

Once I saw a wolf tread a circle in his cage
amid the stench of monkeys, the noise of musty
jungle birds. We threw him bits of doughy
bread but he didn't see us, padding on through
some imagined forest, his nose on blood.
We began to move on in boredom when he jumped
against the bars, snarled, then howled
in rage that long shrill howl that must remind
us of another life. Children screamed and ran,
their parents passing them in terror – the summer
day became hard and brittle. I stooped there
and watched his anger until the keeper
came with a Flash Gordon gun and shot him full
of dope. He grew smaller and sputtered into sleep.

REVERIE

He thinks of the dead. But they
appear as dead – beef-colored and torn.

There is a great dull music
in the ocean that lapses into seascape.

The girl bends slowly
from the waist. Then stoops.

In high school Brutus
died upon a rubber knife.

Lift the smock. The sun
light stripes her back. A *fado* wails.

In an alley in Cambridge. Beneath
a party's noise. Bottle caps stuck to them.

FOX FARM

In the pasture a shire
whose broad muscles once
drew a hayrake,
a plough,
can't hold the weight of his great
head and neck –
he will be fed to the foxes.

And the Clydesdales and saddle nags
that stray along the fence
with limps and sagging bellies,
with rheumy eyes (one
has no tail).

But the foxes
not having known field
or woods,
bred, born in long rows of hutches,
will die to adorn some
woman's neck.

NIGHTMARE

Through the blinds
a white arm caresses a vase of zinnias

beneath the skin
of a pond the laughter of an eye

in the loft
the hot straw suffocates
the rafters become snakes

through the mow door
three deer in a cool pasture
nibbling at the grass
mercurous in the moon.

CREDO, AFTER E.P.

Go, my songs
to the young and insolent,
speak the love of final things –
do not betray me
as a dancer, drunk,
is dumb to his clumsiness.

DUSK

Dusk over the lake,
clouds floating
heat lightning
a nightmare behind branches;
from the swamp
the odor of cedar and fern,
the long circular
wail of the loon –
the plump bird aches for fish
for night to come down.

Then it becomes so dark
and still
that I shatter the moon with an oar.

LISLE'S RIVER

Dust followed our car like a dry brown cloud.
At the river we swam, then in the canoe passed
downstream toward Manton; the current carried us
through cedar swamps, hot fields of marsh grass
where deer watched us and the killdeer shrieked.
We were at home in a thing that passes.
And that night, camped on a bluff, we ate eggs
and ham and three small trout; we drank too much
whiskey and pushed a burning stump down the bank –
it cast hurling shadows, leaves silvered and darkened,
the crash and hiss woke up a thousand birds.

Now, tell me, other than lying between some woman's legs,
what joy have you had since, that equaled this?

THREE NIGHT SONGS

I

He waits to happen with the clear
reality of what he thinks about –
to be a child who wakes beautifully,
a man always in the state of waking
to a new room, or at night, waking
to a strange room with snow outside,
and the moon beyond glass,
in a net of branches,
so bright and clear and cold.

II

Moving in liquid dark,
night's water,
a flat stone sinking,
wobbling toward bottom;
and not to wait there for morning,
to see the sun up through the water,
but to freeze until another glacier comes.

III

The mask riddles itself,
there's heat through the eye slits,
a noise of breathing,
the plaster around the mouth is wet;
and the dark takes no effort,
dark against deeper dark,
the mask dissembles,
a music comes to the point of horror.

CARDINAL

That great tree covered with snow
until its branches droop,
the oak, that keeps its leaves through winter
(in spring a bud breaks the stem),
has in its utmost branch
a cardinal,
who brushing snow aside, pauses for an instant
then plummets toward earth
until just above a drift he opens his wings
and brakes, fluttering
in a cloud of snow he pushed aside.

"THIS IS COLD SALT..."

This is cold salt
a pulled tooth
the freshly set bone:
the girl who left my bed this morning,
who smiled last night as her slip
floated to the floor,
my Roselita,
today up on Amsterdam Avenue
I saw her with her Manuelo.

JOHN SEVERIN WALGREN, 1874–1962

Trees die of thirst or cold
or when the limit's reached;
in the hole in the elm
the wood is soft and punky –
it smells of the water of a vase
after the flowers are dumped.

You were so old we could not weep;
only the blood of the young,
those torn off earth in a night's sickness,
the daughter lying beside you
who became nothing so long ago –
she moves us to terror.

GARDEN

Standing at the window at night
my shadow is the length of the garden –
I move a huge arm and
cause plants to spring up,
tomatoes to ripen.
My head is as large
as a strawberry bed and I can
cup two bales of straw in one hand.
I take pride in this strength,
fed by light and darkness,
wielded against my father's garden –
a lord of shadows.

HORSE

A
quarter horse, no rider
canters through the pasture

thistles raise soft purple burrs
her flanks are shiny in the sun

I whistle and she runs
almost sideways toward me

the oats in my hand are sweets to her:

dun mane furling in its breeze,
her neck
corseted with muscle,
wet teeth friendly against my hand –
how can I believe
you ran under a low maple limb
to knock me off?

MALEDICTION

Man's not a singing animal,
his tongue hangs from a wall –
    pinch the stone
    to make a moan
    from the throat
    a single note
    breaks the air
    so bare and harsh
    birds die.

He's crab-necked from cold,
song splits his voice
like a lake's ice cracking.
His heart's a rock,
a metronome, a clock,
a foghorn drone of murder.

God, curse this self-maimed beast,
the least of creatures,
rivet his stone with worms.

WORD DRUNK

I think of the twenty thousand poems of Li Po
and wonder, do words follow me or I them –
a word drunk?
I do not care about fine phrases,
the whoring after honor,
the stipend, the gift, the grant –
but I would feed on an essence
until it yields to me my own dumb form –
the weight raw, void of intent;
to see behind the clarity of my glass
the birth of new creatures
suffused with light.

YOUNG BULL

This bronze ring punctures
the flesh of your nose,
the wound is fresh
and you nuzzle the itch
against a fence post.
Your testicles are fat and heavy
and sway when you shake off flies;
the chickens scratch about your feet
but you do not notice them.

Through lunch I pitied
you from the kitchen window –
the heat, pained fluid of August –
but when I came with cold water
and feed, you bellowed and heaved
against the slats wanting to murder me.

PARK AT NIGHT

Unwearied
the coo and choke
of doves
the march of stone
an hour before dawn.

Trees caged to the waist
wet statues
the trickling of water —
in the fountain
floating across the lamp
a leaf
some cellophane.

GOING BACK

How long, stone, did it take
to get that fat?

The rain made the furrow a rut
and then among the mint and nettles
you make your appearance.

Sink again, you might cover bones.

HITCHHIKING

Awake:
the white hand of
my benefactor
drums on the seat
between us.
The world had become orange
in the rearview mirror
of a '55 Pontiac.
The road was covered with bugs
and mist coiled around
great house-sized rocks
and in the distance buried them.
Village. Passed three limp
gas stations then one
whose windows exploded with fire.
My mouth was filled with plastic cups.
Final item:
breakfast, nurtured
by a miraculous hatred.

SOUND

At dawn I squat on the garage
with snuff under a lip
to sweeten the roofing nails –
my shoes and pant cuffs
are wet with dew.
In the orchard the peach trees
sway with the loud
weight of birds, green fruit, yellow haze.
And my hammer – the cold head taps,
then swings its first full arc;
the sound echoes against the barn,
muffled in the loft,
and out the other side, then lost
in the noise of the birds
as they burst from the trees.

DEAD DEER

Amid pale green milkweed, wild clover,
a rotted deer
curled, shaglike,
after a winter so cold
the trees split open.
I think she couldn't keep up with
the others (they had no place
to go) and her food,
frozen grass and twigs,
wouldn't carry her weight.

Now from bony sockets,
she stares out on this
cruel luxuriance.

LI HO

Li Ho of the province of Honan
      (not to be confused with the god Li Po
      of Kansu or Szechwan
      who made twenty thousand verses),
Li Ho, whose mother said,
"My son daily vomits up his heart,"
mounts his horse and rides
to where a temple lies as lace among foliage.
His youth is bargained
for some poems in his saddlebag –
his beard is gray. Leaning
against the flank of his horse he considers
the flight of birds
but his hands are heavy. (Take this cup,
he thinks, fill it, I want to drink again.)
Deep in his throat, but perhaps it is a bird,
he hears a child cry.

COMPLAINT

Song, I am unused to you –
When you come
your voice is behind trees
calling another by my name.

So little of me comes out to you
I cannot hold your weight –
I bury you in sleep
or pour more wine, or lost in another's
music, I forget that you ever spoke.

If you come again, come with
Elias! Elias! Elias!
If only once the summons were a roar,
a pillar of light,
I would not betray you.

RETURN

The sun's warm against the slats of the granary,
a puddle of ice in the shadow of the steps;
a bluetick hound lopes
across the winter wheat –
fresh green, cold green.
The windmill, long out of use,
screeches and twists in the wind.
A spring day too loud for talk
when bones tire of their flesh
and want something better.

LOCATIONS

to Herbert Weisinger

1968

WALKING

Walking back on a chill morning past Kilmer's Lake
into the first broad gully, down its trough
and over a ridge of poplar, scrub oak, and into
a larger gully, walking into the slow fresh warmth
of midmorning to Spider Lake where I drank
at a small spring remembered from ten years back;
walking northwest two miles where another gully
opened, seeing a stump on a knoll where my father
stood one deer season, and tiring of sleet and cold
burned a pine stump, the snow gathering fire-orange
on a dull day; walking past charred stumps blackened
by the '81 fire to a great hollow stump near a basswood
swale – I sat within it on a November morning
watching deer browse beyond my young range of shotgun
and slug, chest beating hard for killing –
into the edge of a swale waist-high with ferns,
seeing the quick movement of a blue racer,
and thick curl of the snake against a birch log,
a pale blue with nothing of the sky in it,
a fleshy blue, blue of knotted veins in an arm;
walking to Savage's Lake where I ate my bread
and cheese, drank cool lake water, and slept for a while,
dreaming of fire, snake and fish and women in white
linen walking, pinkish warm limbs beneath white linen;
then walking, walking homeward toward Well's Lake,
brain at boil now with heat, afternoon glistening
in yellow heat, dead dun-brown grass, windless,
with all distant things shimmering, grasshoppers, birds
dulled to quietness; walking a log road near a cedar swamp
looking cool with green darkness and whine of mosquitoes,
crow's caw overhead, Cooper's hawk floating singly

in mateless haze; walking dumbly, footsore, cutting
into evening through sumac and blackberry brambles,
onto the lake road, feet sliding in the gravel,
whippoorwills, night birds wakening, stumbling to lake
shore, shedding clothes on sweet moss; walking
into syrupy August moonless dark, water cold, pushing
lily pads aside, walking out into the lake with feet
springing on mucky bottom until the water flows overhead;
sinking again to walk on the bottom then buoyed up,
walking on the surface, moving through beds of reeds,
snakes and frogs moving, to the far edge of the lake
then walking upward over the basswood and alders, the field
of sharp stubble and hay bales, toward the woods,
floating over the bushy crests of hardwoods and tips
of pine, barely touching in miles of rolling heavy dark,
coming to the larger water, there walking along the troughs
of waves folding in upon themselves; walking to an island,
small, narrow, sandy, sparsely wooded, in the middle
of the island in a clump of cedars a small spring
which I enter, sliding far down into a deep cool
dark endless weight of water.

SUITE TO FATHERS

for Denise Levertov

I

I think that night's our balance,
our counterweight – a blind woman
we turn to for nothing but dark.

•••

In Val-Mont I see a slab of parchment,
a black quill pen in stone.
In a sculptor's garden
there was a head made from stone,
large as a room, the eyes neatly hooded
staring out with a crazed somnolence
fond of walled gardens.

•••

The countesses arch like cats in châteaux.
They wake up as countesses and usually sleep with counts.
Nevertheless he writes them painful letters,
thinking of Eleanor of Aquitaine, Gaspara Stampa.
With Kappus he calls forth the stone in the rose.

•••

In Egypt the dhows sweep the Nile
with ancient sails. I am in Egypt,
he thinks, this Baltic jew – it is hot,
how can I make bricks with no straw?
His own country rich with her food and slaughter,
fit only for sheep and generals.

♦♦♦

He thinks of the coffin of the East,
of the tiers of dead in Venice,
those countless singulars.
At lunch, the baked apple too sweet with kirsch
becomes the tongues of convent girls at gossip,
under the drum and shadow of pigeons
the girl at promenade has almond in her hair.

♦♦♦

From Duino, beneath the mist,
the green is so dark and green it cannot bear itself.
In the night, from black paper
I cut the silhouette of this exiled god,
finding him as the bones of a fish in stone.

II

In the cemetery the grass is pale,
fake green as if dumped from Easter baskets,
from overturned clay and the deeper marl
which sits in wet gray heaps by the creek.
There are no frogs, death drains there.
Landscape of glass, perhaps Christ
will quarry you after the worms.
The newspaper says caskets float in leaky vaults.
Above me, I feel paper birds.
The sun is a brass bell.
This is not earth I walk across
but the pages of some giant magazine.

•••

Come song,
allow me some eloquence,
good people die.

•••

The June after you died
I dove down into a lake,
the water turned to cold, then colder,
and ached against my ears.
I swam under a sunken log then paused,
letting my back rub against it,
like some huge fish with rib cage
and soft belly open to the bottom.
I saw the light shimmering far above
but did not want to rise.

•••

It was so far up from the dark —
once it was night three days,
after that four, then six and over again.
The nest was torn from the tree,
the tree from the ground,
the ground itself sinking torn.
I envied the dead their sleep of rot.
I was a fable to myself,
a speech to become meat.

III

Once in Nevada I sat on a boulder at twilight –
I had no ride and wanted to avoid the snakes.
I watched the full moon rise a fleshy red
out of the mountains, out of a distant sandstorm.
I thought then if I might travel deep enough
I might embrace the dead as equals,
not in their separate stillness as dead, but in music
one with another's harmonies.
The moon became paler,
rising, floating upward in her arc
and I with her, intermingled in her whiteness,
until at dawn again she bloodied
herself with earth.

•••

In the beginning I trusted in spirits,
slight things, those of the dead in procession,
the household gods in mild delirium
with their sweet round music and modest feasts.
Now I listen only to that hard black core,
a ball harsh as coal, rending for light
far back in my own sour brain.

•••

The tongue knots itself
a cramped fist of music,
the oracle a white-walled room of bone
that darkens now with a greater dark;

and the brain a glacier of blood,
inching forward, sliding, the bottom
silt covered but sweet,
becoming a river now
laving the skull with coolness –
the leaves on her surface
dipping against the bone.

    ♦♦♦

Voyager, the self the voyage –
dark, let me open your lids.
Night stares down with her great bruised eye.

SUITE TO APPLENESS

I

If you love me drink this discolored wine,
tanning at the edge with the sourness of flowers –
their heads, soldiers', floating as flowers,
heads, necks, owned by gravity now as war
owned them and made them move to law;
and the water is heavier than war, the heads
bobbing freely there with each new wave lap.

•••

And if your arm offends you, cut it off.
Then the leg by walking, tear out the eye,
the trunk, body be eyeless, armless, bodiless.
And if your brain offends you...
If Christ offends you, tear him out,
or if the earth offends you, skin her
back in rolls, nailed to dry
on barnside, an animal skin in sunlight;
or the earth that girl's head,
throwing herself from the asylum roof,
head and earth whirling earthward.

•••

Or if we reoccur with death our humus, heat,
as growths or even mushrooms; on my belly
I sight for them at dead-leaf line –
no better way – thinking there that I hear
the incredible itch of things to grow,
Spring, soon to be billion-jetted.

Earth in the boy's hand, the girl's head,
standing against the granary; earth a green
apple he picked to throw at starlings,
plucked from among green underleaves,
silver leaf bellies burred with fine white hairs;
the apple hurled, hurtling greenly with wet solidity,
earth spinning in upon herself,
shedding her brains and whales and oceans,
her mountains strewn and crushed.

II

In the Quonset shed unloading the fertilizer,
each bag weighing eighty pounds,
muscles ache, lungs choke with heat and nitrogen;
then climbing the ladder of the water tank
to see in the orchard the brightness of apples,
sinking clothed into the icy water, feet thunking
iron bottom, a circle of hot yellow light above.

•••

The old tree, a McIntosh:
sixty-eight bushel last year,
with seventy-three bushel the year before that,
sitting up within it on a smooth branch,
avoiding the hoe, invisible to the ground,
buoyed up by apples, brain still shocked,
warped, shaved into curls of paper,

a wasps' globe of gray paper –
lamina of oil and clouds –
now drawing in greenness, the apples
swelling to heaviness on a hot August afternoon;
to sing, singing, voice cracks at second sing,
paper throat, brain unmoist for singing.

•••

Cranking the pump to loud life,
the wheel three turns to the left,
six hundred feet of pipe lying in the field;
the ground beneath begins shaking, bumping
with the force of coming water, sprinklers whirl,
the ground darkening with spray of flung water.

•••

After the harvest of cabbage the cabbage roots,
an acre of them and the discarded outer leaves,
scaly pale green roots against black soil,
to be forked into piles with the tomato vines;
a warm week later throwing them onto the wagon,
inside the piles the vines and leaves have rotted,
losing shape, into a thick green slime and jelly.

III

Or in the orchard that night
in July: the apple trees too thick
with branches, unpruned, abandoned,
to bear good fruit – the limbs

moving slightly in still air with my drunkenness;
a cloud passed over the moon
sweeping the orchard with a shadow –
the shadow moving thickly across the darkening field,
a moving lustrous dark, toward a darker woodlot.

♦♦♦

Then the night exploded with crows –
an owl or raccoon disturbed a nest –
I saw them far off above the trees,
small pieces of black in the moonlight
in shrill fury circling with caw caw caw,
skin prickling with its rawness
brain swirling with their circling
in recoil moving backward, crushing
the fallen apples with my feet,
the field moving then as the folds
of a body with their caw caw caw.
Young crows opened by owl's beak,
raccoon's claws and teeth,
night opened, brain broken as with a hammer
by weight of blackness and crows,
crushed apples and drunkenness.

♦♦♦

Or Christ bless torn Christ, crows,
the lives of their young
torn from the darkness,
apples and the dead webbed branches
choking the fruit;

night and earth herself
a drunken hammer, the girl's head,
all things bruised or crushed
as an apple.

THE SIGN

There are no magic numbers or magic lives.
He dreams of Sagittarius in a thicket,
dogs yipe at his hooves, the eye of the archer
seaward, his gaze toward impossible things –
bird to be fish, archer and horse a whale
or dolphin; then rears up, canters
away from the shore across a wide field
of fern and honeysuckle brambles
to a woods where he nibbles at small
fresh leeks coming up among dead leaves.

♦♦♦

Strange creature to be thought of,
welded in the skull as unicorn,
hooves, bow, quiver of arrows and beard;
that girl sitting at cliff edge
or beside a brook, how does he take her?
He lifts her up to kiss her,
and at night standing by a stream,
heavy mist up to his flanks,
mist curling and floating through his legs,
a chill comes over him;
she in restless sleep in a small stone cottage.

♦♦♦

Between the scorpion and goat,
three signs –
winter in Cancer and this love of snow.

•••

And contempt for all signs, the nine
spokes of the sun, the imagined belt
of dark or girdle in which night
mantles herself. The stars guide
no one save those at sea
or in the wilderness; avoid what stinks
or causes pain, hate death and cruelty
to any living thing.
You do not need the stars for that.

II

But often at night something asks
the brain to ride, run riderless;
plumed night swirling, brain riding itself
through blackness, crazed with motion,
footless against the earth,
perhaps hooves imagined in lunacy;
through swamps feared even in daytime
at gallop, crashing through poplar
thickets, tamarack, pools of green slime,
withers splattered with mud, breathing
deep in an open marsh in the center of
the great swamp, then running again
toward a knoll of cedar where deer feed,
pausing, stringing the bow, chasing
the deer for miles, crossing a blacktop road
where the hooves clatter.

◆◆◆

On a May night walking home from a tavern
through a village with only three streetlights,
a slip of moon and still air moist with scent of first grass;
to look into the blackness by the roadside,
and in all directions, village, forest,
and field covered with it:

      eighteen miles of black to Traverse City
      thirteen miles of black to Buckley
      nineteen miles of black to Karlin
      twelve miles of black to Walton Junction

◆◆◆

And infinite black above;
earth herself a heavy whirling ball of pitch.
If the brain expands to cover these distances...
stumbling to the porch where the cat
has left an injured snake that hisses with the brain,
the brain rearing up to shed the black
and the snake coiled bleeding at its center.

III

Not centaur nor archer but man,
man standing exhausted at night
beneath a night sky so deep and measureless,
head thrown back he sees his constellation,
his brain fleshes it and draws the lines
which begin to ripple then glimmer,

heave and twist, assume color, rear up,
the head high, the chest and torso gleaming,
beard glistening, flanks strapped with muscle,
hooves stomping in place, stomping night's floor,
rearing again, fading, then regaining terror,
the bow in hand, a strung bow, and arrow fitted,
drawn back, the arrow molten-tipped.
Slay. He only still "slays."
And when the arrow reaches earth I'll die.

＊＊＊

But in morning light, already shrill and hot
by ten, digging a well pit, the sandy earth crumbles
and traps the legs, binding them to earth; then digging
again, driving a shallow well with a sledge,
the well-tip shaded as an arrowhead, sledge hitting
steel with metallic ring and scream; the pump head
and arm bound to pipe, sitting in damp sand
with legs around the pipe pumping the first water
onto my chest and head – head swollen with pain
of last night's sign and leavings of whiskey.

＊＊＊

On another morning, the frost as a sheet
of white stubbled silk soon to melt into greenness,
partridge thumping ground with wings to call their mates,
near a river, thick and turbulent and brown –
a great buck deer, startled
from a thicket, a stag of a thousand stories,

how easily his spread antlers trace a back and bow
not unlike your own, then the arc of him
bounding away into his green clear music.

WAR SUITE

I

The wars: we're drawn to them
as if in fever, we sleepwalk to them,
wake up in full stride of nightmare,
blood slippery, mouth deep in their gore.

•••

Even in *Gilgamesh,* the darker bodies
strewn over stone battlements,
dry skin against rough stone, the sand
sifting through rock face, swollen flesh
covered with it, sand against blackening lips,
flesh covered with it, the bodies
bloating in the heat, then hidden,
then covered; or at an oasis, beneath
still palms, a viper floats toward water,
her soft belly flattened of its weight, tongue
flicking at water beside the faces of the dead,
their faces, chests, pressed to earth, bodies
also flattened, lax with their weight,
now surely groundlings, and the moon
swollen in the night, the sheen
of it on lax bodies and on the water.

•••

Now in Aquitaine, this man is no less dead
for being noble, a knight with a clang
and rasp to his shield and hammer;
air thick with horses,

earth fixed under their moving feet
but bodies falling, sweat and blood
under armor, death blows, sweet knight's
blood flowing, horses screaming, horses
now riderless drinking at a brook, mouths sore
with bits, sweat drying gray on flanks,
noses dripping cool water, nibbling
grass through bits, patches of grass
with the blood still red and wet on them.

II

I sing sixty-seven wars; the war now,
the war for Rapunzel, earth cannot use
her hair, the war of drowning hair
drifting upward as it descends,
the lover holding his cock like
a switchblade, war of
apples and pears beating against the earth,
earth tearing a hole in sky, air to hold
the light it has gathered, river bending
until its back is broken, death a black
carp to swim in our innards.

•••

Grand wars; the final auk poised
on her ice floe, the wolf shot
from a helicopter; that shrill god
in her choir loft among damp wine-colored
crumpled robes, face against a dusty

window, staring out at a black pond
and the floor of a woodlot
covered with ferns – if that wasp
on the pane stings her…
cancer to kill child, child to kill cancer,
nail to enter the wood, the Virgin
to flutter in the air above Rome like a Piper Cub,
giraffe's neck to grow after greener leaves,
bullet to enter an eye, bullet
to escape the skull, bullet to fall
to earth, eye to look for its skull,
skull to burst, belly to find its cage or ribs.

•••

Face down in the pool, his great fatty
heart wants to keep beating; tongue pressed
to rug in a chemical hallway; on a country
road, caught by flashbulb headlights,
he wishes suddenly to be stronger than a car.

III

The elephant to couple in peace,
the porpoise to be free of the microphone;
this page to know a master, a future,
a page with the flesh melodious,
to bring her up through the page, paper-shrouded,
from whatever depth she lies,
dulling her gift, bringing her to song
and not to life.

•••

This death mask to harden before
the face escapes, life passes
down through the neck – the sculptor
turns hearing it rub against the door.

•••

Mind to stay free of madness, of war;
war all howling and stiff-necked dead,
night of mind punctuated with moans and stars,
black smoke moiling, puling mind striped as a zebra,
ass in air madly stalking her lion.

•••

Fire to eat tar, tar to drip,
hare to beat hound
grouse to avoid shot
trout to shake fly
chest to draw breath
breath to force song,
a song to be heard,
remembered and sung.

•••

To come to an opening in a field
without pausing, to move there in a full circle of light;
but night's out there not even behind the glass –
there's nothing to keep her out or in;

73

to walk backward to her, to step
off her edge or become her edge,
to swell and roll in her darkness,
a landlocked sea moving free –
dark and clear within her continent.

AMERICAN GIRL

I

Not a new poem for Helen,
if they were heaped...
but she never wanted a poem,
she whose affections the moment aimed.
And not to sing a new Helen into being
with *t'adores,* anachronistic gymnastics,
to be diligent in praise of her
only to be struck down by her.
Sing then, if song,
after bitter retreat,
on your knees,
as anyone who would love.
My senses led me here
and I had no wit to do otherwise.
Who breathes. Has looked upon. Alone.
In the darkness. Remembers.

•••

Better to sit as a boy did in a still
cool attic in fall, tomatoes left to ripen
in autumn light on newspapers,
sucking his honeyed thumb, the forbidden
magazine across the lap and only
the mind's own nakedness for company;
the lovely photo, almost damp,
as supple and pink to the eye,
a hot country of body
but unknown and distant,
perhaps futureless.

●●●

A child once thought the dead were buried
to bear children: in the morning from his loft
in the fumes of wood smoke and bacon
he watches them dress, their bathing suits drying
by the stove. The water will fill them up.

II

He dreams of Egypt in Sunday School,
the maidens of Ur-of-Chaldea, Bathsheba bathing
on her rooftop, the young virgin brought
to David to warm his hollow bones. And the horror
of Sodom and Gomorrah, Lot's frenzy
with his daughters; women railed against
in Habakkuk and Jeremiah, Isaiah's feverish
wife and Christ and the woman at the well –
to look in lust is to do without doing;
eyes follow the teacher's rump as she leaves the room.

●●●

At sixteen his first whore, youngish
and acrid, sharing with her a yellow room
and a fifth of blackberry brandy;
first frightened with only his shoes on,
then calmed, then pleased, speechlessly
preening and arrogant. They became
blackberry brandy but never sweetly again –
vile in Laramie before dawn through

a darkened bar and up the long backstairs,
on Commerce St. in Grand Rapids shrieking
with gin. He craved some distant cousin
in Sweden he'd never seen, incestuously,
in some flower-strewn woods near the water.

•••

After a New Year's and his first French meal,
enchantée of course pursing her thick lips,
throwing one leg over the other
in the abandonment of sitting down,
throwing off room-length heat beneath layers
of nylon, stuffed with turbot and filet as she is,
splendidly in health, though her only apparent
exercise is screwing, "making the love,"
not gentle-like but as a Mack truck
noses a loading platform.

III

The same "she" seen from a bus
or store window, often too young,
across the subway tracks in pure ozone,
the blond cheerleader with legs
bared to hundreds of eyes.
Always a fool before the coins –
I Ching forcing turmoil, the cauldron.
The fool has eyes and touch,
is mammalian. He lacks all odds,
ruts then is scathed. There's Helen

in a Greek nightclub, a hundred
years old and selling pistachios,
half a century away from any bed –
her face a shucked pecan.

◆◆◆

Near the shore in a bed of reeds
he finally sees her for a moment,
the moon their only witness,
a single white eye;
her face is swirling in the dark,
changing faces a thousand times
then slipping back into black water.

◆◆◆

But they are confections, put-together things
who will not stay in or go out but pause
on the edge of a room or wherever they are,
uncertain of what they are or whether they care.
So are they praised for what they aren't, young,
and blamed for what they haven't, a wilderness
of blood; pitiful creatures, calcined, watery,
with airbrushed bodies and brains.

◆◆◆

I write this out of hard silence
to be rid of it. Not, as once, in love,
chin on breastbone as if the head
by its own dull weight would snap,
a green flower from a green stem.

LULLABY FOR A DAUGHTER

Go to sleep. Night is a coal pit
full of black water –
        night's a dark cloud
full of warm rain.

Go to sleep. Night is a flower
resting from bees –
        night's a green sea
swollen with fish.

Go to sleep. Night is a white moon
riding her mare –
        night's a bright sun
burned to black cinder.

Go to sleep,
night's come,
cat's day,
owl's day,
star's feast of praise,
moon to reign over
her sweet subject, dark.

SEQUENCE

1

The mad have black roots in their brains
around which vessels clot and embrace
each other as mating snakes.

The roots feed on the brain until the brain
is all root – now the brain is gray
and suffocates in its own folds.

The brain grows smaller and beats
against its cage of bone
like a small wet bird.

Let us pity the mad we see every day,
the bird is dying without air and water
and growing smaller,
the air is cold, her beak is sharp,
the beating shriller.

2

He loves her until
tomorrow or until 12:15 AM
when again he assumes the firedrake,
ricochets from the walls
in the exhaustion of kingship;
somewhere in his skull the Bible's leaves
seem turned by another's hand.

The pool table's green felt is earth,
ivory balls, people cracked toward leather holes.

Christ's blood is whiskey. Light is dark.
And light from a cave in whose furnace
three children continue their burning.

3

The dead haloed in gladiolus
and electric organs,
those impossible hurts, trepanations,
the left eye punctured with glass;
he'll go to Canada with his dog,
a truly loved and loving creature –
fish in the water, bear in his den.
Not fox shrinking before foxhound
snaps its neck, horse cowered before crop.

4

In the woods the low red bridge,
under it and above the flowing water,
spiders roost in girder's
rust and scale, flaking to touch.
Swift clear water. Soiled sand,
slippery green moss on rock face.
From the red bridge, years back
he dove into an eddy catching
the river's backward bend and swirl,
wishing not to swim on or in
as a duck and fish
but to be the water herself,
flowing then and still.

COLD AUGUST

The sun had shrunk to a dime,
passing behind the smallest
of clouds; the field was root
bare – shorthorns had grazed
it to leather. August's coldest
day when the green, unlike
its former self, returned to earth
as metal. Then from a swamp
I saw two large shadows floating
across the river, move up the sloping
bank, float swiftly as shadows against
the field toward where I stood.
I looked up as two great red-tailed
hawks passed overhead; for an instant
I felt as prey then wheeled to watch
them disappear in southward course.

NIGHT IN BOSTON

From the roof the night's the color
of a mollusk, stained with teeth and oil –
she wants to be rid of us and go to sea.

And the soot is the odor of brine
and imperishable sausages.

Beneath me from a window I hear "Blue Hawaii."
On Pontchartrain the Rex Club
dances on a houseboat in a storm –
a sot calms the water without wetting a foot.

I'd walk to Iceland, saluting trawlers.
I won't sell the rights to this miracle.

It was hot in Indiana.
The lovers sat on a porch swing, laughing;
a car passed on the gravel road,
red taillights bobbing over the ruts,
dust sweeping the house,
the scent of vetch from the pasture.

Out there the baleen nuzzles his iceberg,
monuments drown in the lava of birdshit.
I scuffle the cinders but the building doesn't shudder –
they've balanced it on a rock.
The Charles floats seaward, bored with history.

Night, cutting you open
I see you're full of sour air
like any rubber ball.

FEBRUARY SWANS

Of the hundred swans in West Bay
not one flies south in winter.
They breathe the dust of snow
swirling in flumes across the water,
white as their whiteness;
bones slighted by hunger
they move through the clots of ice,
heads looped low and tucked to the wind,
looking for fish in the deep greenness of water.

Now in the country, far from the Bay,
from a dark room I see a swan gliding
down the street, larger than a car, silent.
She'll need a fish the size of a human
to feed her hunger, so far from the water.
But there's nothing to eat between those snowbanks.
She looks toward my window. I think:
Go back to the Bay, beautiful thing,
it was thirty below last night.
We gaze at each other until my breath
has glazed the window with frost.

THIN ICE

Now this paste of ash and water;
water slipping over ice, greenish

brown water, white ice, November ice,
thin as glass, shot with air.

The kinglet, soundless, against the yellow
grapeleaves of the arbor, smallest of birds;

shrill day, the blowing, oily Atlantic off
Strong's Neck; the salt smell drifts, blown

through the newish Cape Cod homes.
On such days children fall down wells,

or drown falling through thin first ice,
or fall reaching after the last apple

the picker neglected, the tree leafless,
the apple spoiled anyway by frost; toad freezes,

snake's taken his hole; the cat makes much
shorter trips; dog's bark is louder.

The green has floated from earth, moved south,
or drifted upward at night, invisible to us.

Man walks, throwing off alone thin heat;
this cold's life, death's steamy mark and target.

NATURAL WORLD

1

The earth is almost round. The seas
are curved and hug the earth, both
ends are crowned with ice.

The great Blue Whale swims near
this ice, his heart is warm
and weighs two thousand pounds,
his tongue weighs twice as much;
he weighs one hundred fifty tons.

There are so few of him left
he often can't find a mate;
he drags his six-foot sex
through icy waters,
flukes spread crashing.
His brain is large enough
for a man to sleep in.

2

On Hawk Mountain in Pennsylvania
thousands upon thousands
upon thousands of hawks in migration
have been slaughtered for pleasure.
Drawn north or south in spring and fall:
merlin and kestrel, peregrine, gyrfalcon,
marsh hawk, red-tailed, sharp-tailed,
sharp-shinned, Swainson's hawk,
golden eagle and osprey
slaughtered for pleasure.

MOVING

Not those who have lived here and gone
but what they have left: a worn-out broom,
coat hangers, the legs of a doll,
errors of possession to remind us of ourselves;
but for drunkenness or prayers the walls
collapse in boredom, or any new ecstasy
could hold them up, any moan or caress
or pillow-muffled laugh;
leaving behind as a gift seven rooms of air
once thought cathedral, those imagined
beasts at windows,
her griefs hung from the ceiling for spectacle.

But finally here I am often there
in its vacant shabbiness,
standing back to a window in the dark,
carried by the house as history, a boat,
deeper into a year, into the shadow
of all that happened there.

WHITE

To move into it again, as it was,
      the cows rattling in black stalls,
lowing beneath the wind, the elm
      against the barn, thrashing
there as shadow, all loose boards
      creaking, the moon drawn,
pushed rolling white by wind
      and fat,
      bone white
      snow-and-flour white
      white white
moving into the puddle by the lilacs,
      whiter there, rippling white
beneath dark green twisting petals.
To be silvered by her as the barn,
the grass, the manure pile, the lilacs,
to look again at the reflection
      of her huge eye in water.

AFTER THE ANONYMOUS SWEDISH

Seventeenth century

Deep in the forest there is a pond,
small, shaded by a pine so tall
its shadow crosses her surface.
The water is cold and dark and clear,
let it preserve those who lie at the bottom
invisible to us in perpetual dark.
It is our heaven, this bottomless
water that will keep us forever still;
though hands might barely touch they'll never
wander up an arm in caress or lift a drink;
we'll lie with the swords and bones
of our fathers on a bed of silt and pine needles.
In our night we'll wait
for those who walk the green and turning earth,
our brothers, even the birds and deer,
who always float down to us
with alarmed and startled eyes.

DAWN WHISKEY

Mind follow the nose
this honey of whiskey
I smell through the throat of the bottle.

I hear a wren in the maple
and ten million crickets,
leaf rustle
behind the wren and crickets,
farther back a faint dog bark.

And the glass is cool,
a sweet cedar post that flames so briskly.
Sight bear this honey
through the shell curved around the brain,
your small soft globes
pouring in new light –
remember things that burn with gold
as this whiskey to my tongue.

LEGENDA

This song stays.
No new one carries us, bears
us so high, more swiftly.
And it has no place,
it changes as we change
death drawn to silence
at noon or in still night,
who knows another, wishes one.

None wishes night,
but only one night, one day,
sun and dark at final rest.
River at spring crest,
sky clear blue,
forest at June greenness,
delight of eye in brain fully flowering,
delight of air and light and breath.

A YEAR'S CHANGES

This nadir: the wet hole
in which a beast heaps twigs and bits
of hair, bark and tree skin,
both food and turds mix in the warm
dust its body makes.
In winter the dream of summer,
in summer the dream of sleep,
in spring feasting,
living dreams through the morning.
Fall, my cancer, pared to bone,
I lost my fur, my bite gone dull,
all edges, red and showing; now naked,
February painted with ice, preserve me
in wakefulness – I wait for the rain,
to see a red pine free of snow,
my body uncrabbed, unleashed,
my brain alive.

         •••

In northern Manitoba
a man saw a great bald eagle –
hanging from its neck,
teeth locked in skin and feathers,
the bleached skull of a weasel.

         •••

To sing not instinct or tact,
wisdom,
the song's full stop and death,
but audible things, things moving

at noon in full raw light;
a dog moving around
the tree with the shade –
shade and dog in motion –
alive at noon in full natural light.

◆◆◆

This nightflower, the size of a cat's head –
now moist and sentient –
let it hang there in the dark;
bare beauty asking nothing of us,
if we could graft you to us,
so singular and married to the instant.
But now rest picked, a trillium
never to repeat yourself. Soon enough
you'll know dead air, brief homage,
a sliver of glass in someone's brain.

◆◆◆

Homesick for a dark, clear black space
free of objects; to feel locked as wood
within a tree, a rock deep enough
in earth never to see the surface.

◆◆◆

Snow. There's no earth left under it.
It's too cold to breathe.
Teeth ache, trees crack, the air is bluish.
My breath goes straight up.

This woods is so quiet
that if it weren't for the buffer of trees
I could hear everything on earth.

•••

Only talk. Cloth after the pattern is cut,
discarded, spare wood barely kindling.
At night when the god in you trips,
hee-haws, barks and refuses to come
to tether. Stalk without quarry.
Yesterday I fired a rifle into the lake.

•••

A cold spring dawn
near Parker Creek,
a doe bounding away through
shoulder-high fog
fairly floating,
soundless
as if she were running in a cloud.

•••

That his death was disfigurement:
at impact when light passed
the cells yawned then froze in postures
unlike their former selves, teeth
stuck by the glue of their blood
to windshields, visors. And in the night,

a quiet snowy landscape, three bodies
slump, horribly rended.

•••

Acacia Accidie Accipiter
flower boredom flight
gummy wet pale stemmed
barely above root level
and darkened by ferns;
but hawk
high now spots the car he shot
and left there,
swings low
in narrowing circles,
feeds.

•••

My mouth stuffed up with snow,
nothing in me moves,
earth nudges all things this month.
I've outgrown this shell
I found in a sea of ice —
its drunken convolutions —
something should call me to another life.

•••

Too cold for late May, snow flurries,
warblers tight in their trees, the air
with winter's clearness, dull

pearlish clear under clouds, clean
clear bite of wind, silver maple flexing
in the wind, wind rippling petals,
ripped from flowering crab,
pale pink against green firs, the body
chilled, blood unstirred, thick with frost:
body be snake,
self equal to ground heat,
be wind cold, earth heated,
bend with tree, whip with grass,
move free clean and bright clear.

•••

Night draws on him until he's soft
and blackened, he waits for bones
sharp-edged as broken stone, rubble
in a deserted quarry, to defoliate,
come clean and bare
come clean and dry,
for salt,
he waits for salt.

•••

In the dark I think of the fire,
how hot the shed was when it burned,
the layers of tar paper and dry pine,
the fruit-like billows and blue embers,
the exhausted smell as of a creature
beginning to stink when it has no more to eat.

•••

The doe shot in the back
and just below the shoulder
has her heart and lungs blown out.
In the last crazed seconds she leaves
a circle of blood on the snow.
An hour later we eat
her still-warm liver for lunch,
fried in butter with onions.
In the evening we roast
her loins, and drink two gallons of wine,
reeling drunken and yelling on the snow.
Jon Jackson will eat venison for a month,
he has no job, food or money,
and his pump and well are frozen.

•••

June, sun high, nearly straight above,
all green things in short weak shadow;
clipping acres of pine for someone's
Christmas, forearms sore with trimming,
itching with heat —
drawing boughs away from a trunk
a branch confused with the thick
ugliness of a hognose snake.

•••

Dogged days, dull, unflowering,
the mind petaled in cold wet dark;

outside the orange world is gray,
all things gray turned in upon
themselves in the globed eye of the seer –
gray seen.
But the orange world is orange to itself,
the war continues redly,
the moon is up in Asia,
the dark is only eight thousand miles deep.

♦♦♦

At the edge of the swamp a thorn apple tree
beneath which partridge feed on red berries,
and an elm tipped over in a storm
opening a circle of earth formerly closed,
huge elm roots in a watery place, bare,
wet, as if there were some lid to let
secrets out or a place where the ground
herself begins, then grows outward
to surround the earth; the hole, a black
pool of quiet water, the white roots
of undergrowth. It appears bottomless,
an oracle I should worship at; I want
some part of me to be lost in it and return
again from its darkness, changing the creature,
or return to draw me back to a home.

LOCATIONS

I want this hardened arm to stop
dragging a cherished image.
— RIMBAUD

In the end you are tired of those places,
you're thirty, your only perfect three,
you'll never own another thing.
At night you caress them as if the tongue
turned inward could soothe, head lolling
in its nest of dark, the heart fibrotic,
inedible. Say that on some polar night
an Eskimo thinks of his igloo roof, the blocks
of ice sculptured to keep out air, as the roof
of his skull; all that he is, has seen,
is pictured there – thigh with the texture
of the moon, whale's tooth burnished from use
as nothing, fixtures of place, some delicate
as a young child's ear, close as snails to earth,
beneath the earth as earthworms, farther beneath
as molten rock, into the hollow, vaulted place,
pure heat and pure whiteness,
where earth's center dwells.

You were in Harar but only for a moment,
rifles jostling blue barrels against blue barrels
in the oxcart, a round crater, hot, brown,
a bowl of hell covered with dust.

The angels you sensed in your youth
smelled strongly as a rattlesnake
smells of rotten cucumber, the bear

rising in the glade of ferns of hot fur
and sweat, dry ashes pissed upon.

You squandered your time as a mirror,
you kept airplanes from crashing at your doorstep,
they lifted themselves heavily to avoid your sign,
fizzling like matches in the Atlantic.

You look at Betelgeuse for the splendor
of her name but she inflames another universe.
Our smallest of suns barely touches earth
in the Gobi, Sahara, Mojave, Mato Grosso.

Dumb salvages: there is a box made of wood,
cavernous, all good things are kept there,
and if the branches of ice that claw against the window
become hands, that is their business.

Yuma is an unbearable place.
The food has fire in it as
does the brazero's daughter
who serves the food in an orange dress
the color of a mussel's lip.
Outside it is hot as the crevasse
of her buttocks — perfect body temperature.
You have no idea where your body stops
and the heat begins.

On Lake Superior the undertow swallows
a child and no one notices until evening.
They often drown in the green water

of abandoned gravel pits,
or fall into earth where the crust is thin.

I have tried to stop the war.

You wanted to be a sculptor
creating a new shape that would exalt itself
as the shape of a ball or hand
or breast or dog or hoof,
paw print in snow, each cluster of grapes
vaguely different, bat's wing shaped
as half a leaf, a lake working
against its rim of ground.

You wear yellow this year for Christmas,
the color of Christ's wounds after three days,
the color of Nelse's jacket you wear when writing,
Nelse full of Guckenheimer, sloth, herring, tubercles.

There were sweet places to sleep: beds warmed
by women who get up to work or in the brush
beneath Coit Tower, on picnic tables in Fallon, Nevada,
and Hastings, Nebraska, surrounded by giant curs,
then dew that falls like fine ice upon your face
in a bean field near Stockton, near a waterfall
in the Huron Mountains, memorable sleeps
in the bus stations of San Jose and Toledo, Ohio.

At a roller rink on Chippewa Lake
the skaters move to calliope music.
You watch a motorboat putt by the dock,

they are trolling for bass at night
and for a moment the boat and the two men
are caught in the blue light of the rink,
then pass on slowly upon the black water.

Liquor has reduced you to thumbnails,
keratin, the scales of fish
your ancient relatives,
stranded in a rock pool.

O claritas, sweet suppleness
of breath,
love within a cloud that
blinds us
hear, speak, the world without.

Grove St., Gough St., Heber, Utah,
one in despair, two in disgust,
the third beneath the shadow
of a mountain wall, beyond
the roar of a diesel truck,
faintly the screech of lion.

Self-immolation,
the heaviest of dreams —
you become a charcoal rick
for Christ, for man himself.
They laugh with you as you disappear
lying as a black log upon the cement,
the fire doused by your own blood.

The thunderstorm moved across the lake
in a sheet of rain, the lightning
struck a strawpile, which burned in the night
with hot roars of energy
as in '48 when a jet plane crashed near town,
the pilot parachuting as a leaf through the red sky,
landing miles away, missing the fire.

There was one sun,
one cloud,
two horses running,
a leopard in chase;
only the one sun and a single cloud
a third across her face.
Above, the twelve moons of Jupiter
hissing in cold and darkness.

You worshiped the hindquarters
of beautiful women,
and the beautiful hindquarters of women
who were not beautiful;
the test was the hindquarters
as your father judged cattle.

He is standing behind a plow
in a yellow photograph,
a gangster hat to the back of his head,
in an undershirt with narrow straps,
reins over a shoulder waiting for the photo,
the horses with a foreleg raised,
waiting for the pull with impatience.

The cannon on the courthouse lawn was plugged,
useless against the japs.

In the dark barn
a stillborn calf on the straw,
rope to hooves, its mother bawling
pulled nearly to death.

You've never been across the ocean,
you swept the auditorium with a broom
after the travel lectures and dreamed of going
but the maps have become old, the brain
set on the Mackenzie River, even Greenland
where dentists stalk polar bears from Cessnas.

The wrecked train smelled of camphor,
a bird floating softly above the steam,
the door of the refrigerator car cracked open
and food begins to perish in the summer night.

You've become sure that every year
the sky descends a little,
but there is joy in this pressure,
joy bumping against the lid
like a demented fly, a bird breaking
its neck against a picture window
while outside new gods roll over
in the snow in billowy sleep.

The oil workers sit on the curb
in front of the Blue Moon Bar & Cafe,

their necks red from the sun,
pale white beneath the collars
or above the sleeves; in the distance
you hear the clumping of the wells.
And at a friend's house
there are aunts and uncles, supper plates
of red beans and pork, a guitar is taken
from the wall – in the music
the urge of homesickness, a peach not to be held
or a woman so lovely but not to be touched,
some former shabby home far south of here,
in a warmer place.

Cold cement, a little snow upon it.
Where are the small gods who bless cells?
There are only men. Once you were in a room
with a girl of honey-colored hair,
the yellow sun streamed down air of yellow straw.
You owe it to yourself to despise this place,
the walls sift black powder;
you owe yourself a particular cave.
You wait for her, a stone in loamy stillness,
who will arrive with less pitiful secrets
from sidereal reaches, from other planets of the mind,
who beneath the chamber music of gown and incense
will reflect the damp sweetness of a cave.

At that farm there were so many hogs,
in the center of the pen in the chilled air
he straddles the pig and slits its throat,
blood gushes forth too dark to be blood,

gutted, singed, and scraped into pinkness —
there are too many bowels, the organs
too large, pale sponges that are lungs,
the pink is too pink to understand.

This is earth I've fallen against,
there was no life before this;
        still icon
as if seen through mist,
cold liquid sun, blue falling
from the air,
        foam of ship's prow
cutting water, a green shore beyond
the rocks;
beyond, a green continent.

OUTLYER
& GHAZALS

for Pat Paton

1971

OUTLYER

IN INTERIMS: OUTLYER

Let us open together the last bud of the future.
— APOLLINAIRE

He Halts. He Haw. Plummets.
The snake in the river is belly-up
diamond head caught in crotch of branch,
length wavering yellow with force of water.
Who strangles as this taste of present?
Numen of walking and sleep, knees of snow
as the shark's backbone is gristle.
And if my sister hadn't died in an auto wreck
and had been taken by the injuns
I would have had something to do:
go into the mountains and get her back.

Miranda, I have proof that when people die
they become birds. And I've lost
my chance to go to sea or become a cowboy.
Age narrows me to this window and its
three-week snow. This is Russia and I a clerk.
Miranda throws herself from the window,
the icon clutched to her breasts,
into the snow, over and over.

A world of ruminants, cloven-hoofed,
sum it: is it less worthless for being "in front"?
There are the others, ignorant of us
to a man: says Johnson of Lowell who
wouldn't come to tea who's he sunbitch
and he know armaments and cattle like
a Renaissance prince knew love & daggers

and faintly knew of Dante, or Cecco.
It is a world that belongs to Kipling.

What will I die with in my hand?
A paintbrush (for houses), an M15
a hammer or ax, a book or gavel
                    a candlestick
tiptoeing upstairs.
What will I hold or will I
be caught with this usual thing
that I want to be my heart but
it is my brain and I turn it
over and over and over.

Only miracles should apply,
we have stones enough –
they steal all the heat and trip
everyone even the wary.
Throw stones away.

And
a tricky way of saying something unnecessary
will not do.

The girl standing outside the bus station
in Muskegon, Michigan, hasn't noticed me.
I doubt she reads poetry or if she did
would like it at all or if she liked it
the affection would be casual and temporary.
She would anyway rather ride a horse
than read a poet, read a comic rather than

ride a poet. Sweetie, fifteen minutes
in that black alley bent over the garbage can
with me in the saddle would make
our affections equal. Let's be fair.

I love my dear daughter
her skin is so warm
and if I don't hurt her
she'll come to great harm.
I love my dog Missy
her skin is so warm,
I love all my friends
their skins are so warm,
my dear mother dead father
live sister dead sister
two brothers
their skins are so warm,
I love my lovely wife
her skin is most warm,
and I love my dear self
my skin is so warm,
I come to great harm.
I come to great harm.

I want to be told a children's story
that will stick.
I'm sorry I can't settle for less.
Some core of final delight.
In the funeral parlor my limbs
are so heavy I can't rise.
This isn't me in this nest of silk

but a relative bearing my face and name.
I still wanted to become a cowboy
or bring peace to the Middle East.
This isn't me. I saw Christ this summer
rising over the Absaroka Range.
Of course I was drunk.
I carry my vices to the wilderness.
That faintly blue person there among
the nasturtiums, among crooning relatives
and weeping wife, however, isn't me.

Where. We are born dead.
Our minds can taste this source
until that other death.
A long rain and we are children
and a long snow,
sleeping children in deep snow.

As in interims all journeys end
in three steps
with a mirrored door, beyond it a closet
and a closet wall.
And he wants to write poems to resurrect god,
to raise all buried things the eye
buries and the heart and brain, to
move wild laughter in the throat of death.

A new ax
a new ax
I'm going to play
with my new ax

sharp blue blade
handle of ash.
Then, exhausted, listen
to my new record, Johnny Cash.
Nine dollars in all,
two lovely things to play with
far better and more lasting
than a nine-dollar whore
or two bottles of whiskey.
A new ax and Johnny Cash
sharp blue blade and handle of ash
O the *stream of your blood*
runs as black as the coal.

Saw ghosts not faintly or wispish,
loud they were raising on burly arms
at midday, witches' Sunday in full light,
murder in delight, all former dark things
in noonlight, all light things love
we perform at night and fuck as war wounds
rub, and sigh as others sighed, blind
in delight to the world outside the window.

When I began to make false analogies
between animals & humans, then countries,
Russia is like America and America like Russia,
the universe is the world and the world
a university, the teacher is a crayfish,
the poem is a bird and a housefly, a pig
without a poke, a flame and an oilcan,
a woman who never menstruates, a woman

without glands who makes love by generalized
friction; then I went to the country
to think of precision, O the moon
is the width of a woman's thigh.

The Mexican girl about fourteen years old
in the 1923 *National Geographic* found in the attic
when we thought the chimney was on fire and I stood
on the roof with snow falling looking down into
the black hole where the fire roared at the bottom.
The girl: lying in the Rio Grande in a thin
wet shift, water covering back between breasts
and buttocks but then isolate the buttocks
in the muddy water, two graceful melons from the deep
in the Rio Grande, to ride them up to the river's source
or down to the sea, it wouldn't matter, or I would
carry her like a pack into some fastness like
the Sawtooth Mountains. The melon butter of her
in water, myself in the cloudy brown water
as a fish beneath her.

All falseness flows: you would rust
in jerks, hobbles; they, dewlaps,
sniff eglantine and in mint-cleared voices
not from dark but in puddles over cement,
an inch-deep of watery mud: all falseness
flows; comes now, where should it rest?
Merlin, as Merlin, *le cri de Merlin,*
whose shores are never watched, as women
have no more than one mouth staring
at the ground; repeat now, from what cloud

or clouds or country, countries in dim sleep,
pure song, mouthless, as if a church buried
beneath the sea – one bell tower standing
and one bell; staring for whom at ground's length,
elbows in ground, stare at me now: she grows
from the tree half-vine and half-woman
and haunts all my nights, as music can
that uses our tendons as chords, bowels to hurtle
her gifts; myths as Arcturus, Aldebaran
pictured as colored in with blood,
her eyes were bees and in her hair ice
seemed to glisten, drawn up as plants, the snake
wrapped around the crucifix knows, glass knows,
and O song, meal is made of us not even for small gods
who wait in the morning; dark pushes with no
to and fro, over and under, we who serve her
as canticles for who falls deeper, *breaks away,*
knows praise other than our own: sing.
Merely land and heavily drawn away from the sea
long before us, green has begun, every crevasse, kelp,
bird dung, froth of sea, foam over granite, wet
sea rose and roar of Baltic: who went from continent
to island, as wolves or elk would at night,
sea ice as salted glass, slight lid, mirror over
dark; as Odin least of all gods, with pine smell
of dark and animals crossed in winter
with whales butting shores,
dressed without heat in skins; said Christ who came
late, nothing to be found here, lovers of wood
not stone, north goes over and down, farthest from sun,
aloud in distance white wolf, whiter bear

with red mouth; they can eat flesh and nothing else.

    white winter

    white snow

    black trees

    green boughs

    over us

Arctic sun, one wildflower in profusion,
grass is blue, sterile fishless lake in rock
and northern lights shimmering, crackling.
As a child in mourning, mourned for, knows
how short and bittersweet, not less for saying again,
the child singing knows, near death, it is so alive,
brief and sweet, earth scarcely known, small
songs made of her, how large as hawk or tree,
only a stone lives beyond sweet things:
so that the sea raises herself not swallows
but pushed by wind and moon destroys them;
only dark gives light, Apollo, Christ,
only a blue and knotted earth broken by green
as high above gods see us in our sleeping end.
We know no other, curled as we are here,
sleep over earth, tongues, fog, thunder, wars.
Christ raises. Islands from the sea, see people come.
Clear your speech, it is all that we have,
aloud and here and now.

TRADER

I traded a girl
two apples for an orange.
I hate citrus
but she was beautiful.
As lovers we were rotten –
this was before the sexual revolution –
and we only necked and pawed,
"Don't write below the lines!"
But now she's traded
that child's red mitten
I only touched
for a stovepipe hat,
four children,
and a milkman husband.
Soon I learn there will be no milkmen
and she'll want to trade again.
Stop. I won't take a giant Marianas
trench for two red apples.
You've had your orange
now lie in it.

HOSPITAL

Someone is screaming almost in Morse
code, three longs, a short, three
longs again. Man, woman, or animal?

Pale-blue room. How many have died
here and will I with my ears drummed
to pain with three longs, one short, three longs?

It's never a yelp, it starts
far back in the throat
with three longs, a short, three longs.

All beasts everywhere listen to this.
It must be music to the gods —
three longs, one short, three longs.

I don't know who it is,
a beautiful woman with a lion's lungs
screaming three longs, one short, three longs?

COWGIRL

The boots were on the couch and had
manure on their heels and tips.

The cowgirl with vermilion udders and ears
that tasted of cream pulled on her jeans.

The saddle is not sore and the crotch with
its directionless brain is pounded by hammers.

Less like flowers than grease fittings women
win us to a life of holes, their negative space.

I don't know you and won't. You look at my hairline
while I work, conscious of history, in a bottomless lake.

Thighs that are indecently strong and have won the West,
I'll go back home where women are pliant as marshmallows.

DRINKING SONG

I want to die in the saddle. An enemy of civilization
I want to walk around in the woods, fish and drink.

I'm going to be a child about it and I can't help it, I was
born this way and it makes me very happy to fish and drink.

I left when it was still dark and walked on the path to the
river, the Yellow Dog, where I spent the day fishing and drinking.

After she left me and I quit my job and wept for a year and
all my poems were born dead, I decided I would only fish and drink.

Water will never leave earth and whiskey is good for the brain.
What else am I supposed to do in these last days but fish and drink?

In the river was a trout, and I was on the bank, my heart in my
chest, clouds above, she was in NY forever and I, fishing and drinking.

AWAKE

Limp with night fears: hellebore, wolfsbane,
Marlowe is daggered, fire, volts, African vipers,
the grizzly the horses sensed, the rattlesnake
by the mailbox – how he struck at thrown rocks,
black water, framed by police, wanton wife,
I'm a bad poet broke and broken at thirty-two,
a renter, shot by mistake, airplanes and trains,
half-mast hard-ons, a poisoned earth, sun will
go out, car break down in a blizzard,
my animals die, fistfights, alcohol, caskets,
the hammerhead gliding under the boat near
Loggerhead Key, my soul, my heart, my brain,
my life so interminably struck with an ax
as wet wood splints bluntly, mauled into
sections for burning.

GHAZALS

NOTES ON THE GHAZALS

Poems are always better than a bloody turkey foot in the mailbox. Few would disagree. Robert Creeley once said, partly reconstituting Olson, "Form is never more than an extension of content." True and sage. We choose what suits us and will not fairly wear what doesn't fit. Don't try to bury a horse in a human coffin, no matter how much you loved the horse, or stick some mute, lovely butterfly or luna moth in a damp cavern. I hate to use the word, but form must be an "organic" revelation of content or the poem, however otherwise lively, will strike us false or merely tricky, an exercise in wit, crochet, pale embroidery.

The ghazal is an antique form dating from the thirteenth century and practiced by hundreds of poets since in languages as varied as Urdu, Arabic, Pashto, Turkish, Persian, German, French, and Spanish. Even Goethe and Schlegel wrote ghazals. Among my own contemporaries, Adrienne Rich has been especially successful with the form. I have not adhered to the strictness of metrics and structure of the ancient practitioners, with the exception of using a minimum of five couplets. The couplets are not related by reason or logic and their only continuity is made by a metaphorical jump. Ghazals are essentially lyrics and I have worked with whatever aspect of our life now that seemed to want to enter my field of vision. Crude, holy, natural, political, sexual. After several years spent with longer forms I've tried to regain some of the spontaneity of the dance, the song unencumbered by any philosophical apparatus, faithful only to its own music.

—*J.H.*
1971

I

Unbind my hair, she says. The night is white and warm,
the snow on the mountains absorbing the moon.

We have to get there before the music begins, scattered,
elliptical, needing to be drawn together and sung.

They have dark green voices and listening, there are birds,
coal shovels, the glazed hysteria of the soon-to-be-dead.

I suspect Jesus *will* return and the surprise will be
fatal. I'll ride the equator on a whale, a giraffe on land.

Even stone when inscribed bears the ecstatic. Pressed to
some new wall, ungiving, the screams become thinner.

Let us have the tambourine and guitars and forests, fruit,
and a new sun to guide us, a holy book, tracked in new blood.

II

I load my own shells and have a suitcase of pressed
cardboard. Naturally I'm poor and picturesque.

My father is dead and doesn't care if his vault leaks,
that his casket is cheap, his son a poet and a liar.

All the honest farmers in my family's past are watching
me through the barn slats, from the corncrib and hogpen.

Ghosts demand more than wives & teachers. I'll make a
"V" of my two books and plow a furrow in the garden.

And I want to judge the poetry table at the County Fair.
A new form, poems stacked in pyramids like prize potatoes.

This county agent of poetry will tell poets, "More potash
& nitrogen, the rows are crooked and the field limp, depleted."

III

The alfalfa was sweet and damp in fields where shepherds
lay once and rams strutted and Indians left signs of war.

He harnesses the horses drawing the wagon of wheat toward
the road, ground froze, an inch of sifting snow around their feet.

She forks the hay into the mow, in winter is a hired girl
in town and is always tired when she gets up for school.

Asleep again between peach rows, drunk at midmorning and something
conclusive is needed, a tooth pulled, a fistfight, a girl.

Would any god come down from where and end a small war between
two walls of bone, brain veering, bucking in fatal velocity?

IV

Near a brown river with carp no doubt pressing their
round pursed mouths to the river's bed. Tails upward.

Watching him behind his heifer, standing on a milk
stool, flies buzzing and sister cows swishing tails.

In the tree house the separate nickels placed in her hand.
Skirt rises, her dog yelps below and can't climb ladders.

River and barn and tree. Field where wheat is scarcely high
enough to hide, in light rain knees on pebbles and March mud.

In the brain with Elinor and Sonia, Deirdre of course
in dull flare of peat and Magdalen fresh from the troops.

I want to be old, and old, young. With these few bodies at
my side in a creel with fresh ferns & flowers over them.

V

Yes yes yes it was the year of the tall ships
and the sea owned more and larger fish.

Antiquarians know that London's gutters were
pissed into openly and daggers worn by whores.

Smart's Jeoffry had distant relatives roaming
the docks hungry for garbage at dawn. Any garbage.

O Keats in Grasmere, walking, walking. Tom
is dead and this lover is loverless, loving.

Wordsworth stoops, laughs only once a month and then
in private, mourns a daughter on another shore.

But Keats's heart, Keats in Italy, Keats's heart
Keats how I love thee, I love thee John Keats.

VI

Now changed. None come to Carthage. No cauldrons, all love
comes without oily sacraments. Skin breathes cooler air.

And light was there and two cliff swallows hung and swooped
for flies, audible heat from the field where steers fed.

I'm going to Stonehenge to recant, or from the manure pile
behind this shed I'm going to admit to a cow that I've lied.

He writes with a putty knife and goo, at night the North Star
hangs on the mountain peak like a Christmas ornament.

On the table the frozen rattlesnake thaws, the perfect club!
The perfect crime! Soon now to be skinned for my hatband.

VII

Says he, "Ah Edward I too have a dark past of manual labor."
But now Trivium Charontis seem to want me for Mars.

If her thighs weigh 21 pounds apiece what do her lips weigh?
Do that trick where you touch your toes. Do that right now.

The bold U.S.A. cowpoke in Bozeman, Montana, hates hippies,
cuts off their hair, makes $200 a month, room and board.

We want the sow bear that killed Clark's sheep to go away.
She has two cubs but must die for her terrible appetite.

Girl-of-my-dreams if you'll be mine I'll give up poetry
and be your index finger, lapdog, donkey, obvious unicorn.

VIII

The color of a poppy and bruised, the subalpine green that
ascends the mountainside from where the eagle looked at sheep.

Her sappy brain fleers, is part of the satin shirt (Western) she
wears, chartreuse with red scarf. Poeet he says with two *ees*!

The bull we frighten by waving our hats bellows, his pecker
lengthens touching the grass, he wheels, foam from the mouth.

How do we shoot those things that don't even know they're animals
grazing and stalking in the high meadow: puma elk grizzly deer.

When he pulled the trigger the deer bucked like a horse, spine
broken, grew pink in circles, became a lover kissing him goodnight.

IX

He said the grizzly sat eating the sheep and when the bullet
struck tore the sheep in two, fell over backward dead.

With her mouth warm or cold she remains a welcome mat, a hole
shot through it many years ago in Ohio. Hump. Hemp treaded.

Is there an acre left to be allotted to each man & beast so
they might regard each other on hands and knees behind fences?

The sun straight above was white and aluminum and the trout
on the river bottom watched his feet slip clumsily on the rocks.

I want an obscene epitaph, one that will disgust the Memorial
Day crowds so that they'll indignantly topple my gravestone.

X

Praise me at Durkheim Fair where I've never been, hurling
grenade wursts at those who killed my uncle back in 1944.

Nothing is forgiven. The hurt child is thirty-one years old
and the girl in the pale blue dress walks out with another.

Where love lies. In the crawl space under the back porch
thinking of the aunt seen shedding her black bathing suit.

That girl was rended by the rapist. I'll send her a healing
sonnet in heaven. Forgive us. Forgive us. Forgive us.

The moon I saw through her legs beneath the cherry tree had
no footprints on it and a thigh easily blocked out its light.

Lauren Hutton has replaced Norma Jean, Ava Gardner, Lee Remick
and Vanessa Redgrave in my Calvinist fantasies. Don't go away.

XI

The brain opens the hand which touches that spot, clinically
soft, a member raises from his chair and insists upon his rights.

In some eye bank a cornea is frozen in liquid nitrogen. One day
my love I'll see your body from the left side of my face.

Half the team, a Belgian mare, was huge though weak. She died
convulsively from the 80-volt prod, still harnessed to her mate.

Alvin C. shot the last wolf in the Judith Basin after a four-year
hunt, raising a new breed of hounds to help. Dressed out 90 lbs.

When it rains I want to go north into the taiga, and before I
freeze in arid cold watch the reindeer watch the northern lights.

XII

Says Borges in *Ficciones,* "I'm in hell. I'm dead," and the dark
is glandular and swells about my feet concealing the ground.

Let us love the sun, little children but it is around too
much to notice and has no visible phases to care about.

Two pounds of steak eaten in deference to a tequila hangover.
His sign is that of a pig, a thousand-pound Hampshire boar.

Some would say her face looked homely with that thing sticking
out of it as if to feed her. Not I, said Wynken, not I.

The child is fully clothed but sits in the puddle madly
slapping the warm water on which the sun ripples and churns.

XIII

The night is thin and watery; fish in the air
and moonglint off her necklace of human teeth.

Bring O bring back my Bonnie and I'll return yours
with interest and exhaustion. I'm stuck between those legs.

Dangers of drugs: out in the swamp's middle he's stoned
and a bear hound mammothly threatens. Dazed with fright.

Marcia I won't go to Paris – too free with your body –
it's mine it's mine it's mine not just everyone's.

Now in this natal month Christ must be in some distant
nebula. O come down right now and be with us.

In the hole he fell in, a well pit, yellow jackets stung
him to death. Within minutes death can come by bees.

XIV

That heartless finch, botulinal. An official wheeze passes through
the screen door into the night, the vision of her finally dead.

I've decided here in Chico, Montana, that Nixon isn't president
and that that nasty item, Agnew, is retired to a hamster farm.

And that those mountains hold no people but geologists
spying on each other, and beasts spying on the geologists.

Mule deer die from curiosity — what can that thing be
wandering around with a stick, forgotten from last year?

Some tourists confuse me for an actual cowboy, ecstasy in
deceit, no longer a poet but a bona fide paper buckaroo.

I offer a twenty-one-gun salute to the caress as the blackflies buzz
around me and the rotting elk hides. The true source of the stink.

XV

Why did this sheep die? The legs are thin, stomach hugely
bloated. The girl cries and kicks her legs on the sofa.

The new marvels of language don't come up from the depths
but from the transparent layer, the soiled skin of things.

In London for puissant literary reasons he sits with the other
lost ones at a Soho striptease show. An endless oyster bar.

We'll need miracles of art and reason to raise these years
which are tombstones carved out of soap by the world's senators.

We'll have to move out at dawn and the dew is only a military
metaphor for the generally felt hidden–behind–bushes sorrow.

XVI

It is an hour before dawn and even prophets sleep
on their beds of gravel. Dreams of fish & hemlines.

The scissors moves across the paper and through
the beard. It doesn't know enough or when to stop.

The bear tires of his bicycle but he's strapped on
with straps of silver and gold straps inlaid with scalps.

We are imperturbable as deer whose ancestors saw the last
man and passed on the sweet knowledge by shitting on graves.

Let us arrange to meet sometime in transit, we'll all take
the same train perhaps, Cendrars's Express or the defunct Wabash.

Her swoon was officially interminable with unconvincing
geometric convulsions, no doubt her civic theater experience.

XVII

O Atlanta, roseate dawn, the clodhoppers, hillbillies, rednecks,
drunken dreams of murdering blacks; the gin mills still.

Our fried chicken and Key lime pie and rickets. To drain all
your swamps and touch a match, Seminoles forbidden drink.

Save the dogs everywhere. In France by actual count, Count
Blah Blah shot 885 pheasants in one day, his personal record.

There was a story of a lost child who remained lost & starved
to death hiding in a hollow log from both animals and searchers.

Cuba is off there beyond the Tortugas, forever invisible; Isle
of Pines where Crane wept, collecting tons of starfish and eels.

Her love was committed to horses and poets weighing less than
150 lbs. I weigh 200 and was not allowed into her Blue Fuck Room.

XVIII

I told the dark-haired girl to come down out of the apple
tree and take her medicine. In a dream I told her so.

We're going to have to do something about the night. The tissue
won't restore itself in the dark. I feel safe only at noon.

Waking. Out by the shed, their home, the Chicano cherry pickers
sing hymns on a hot morning, three guitars and a concertina.

We don't need dime-store surrealists buying objects to write
about or all this up-against-the-wall nonsense in *Art News*.

Even in the wilderness, in Hell Roaring Creek Basin, in this
grizzly kingdom, I fear stepping into a hidden missile silo.

My friend has become crippled, back wrenched into an "S" like
my brain. We'll go to Judah to wait for the Apocalypse.

XIX

We were much saddened by Bill Knott's death.
When he reemerged as a hospital orderly we were encouraged.

Sad thoughts of different cuts of meat and how I own no
cattle and am not a rancher with a freezer full of prime beef.

A pure plump dove sits on the wire as if two wings emerged
from a russet pear, head tucked into the sleeping fruit.

Your new romance is full of nails hidden from the saw's teeth,
a board under which a coral snake waits for a child's hand.

I don't want to die in a foreign land and was only in one
once, England, where I felt near death in the Cotswolds.

The cattle walked in the shallow water and birds flew
behind them to feed on the disturbed insects.

XX

Some sort of rag of pure language, no dictums but a bell
sound over clear water, beginning day no. 245 of a good year.

The faces made out of leaves and hidden within them, faces
that don't want to be discovered or given names by anyone.

There was a virgin out walking the night during the plague when
the wolves entered Avila for carrion. The first took her neck.

The ninth month when everything is expected of me and nothing
can be told – September when I sit and watch the summer die.

She knelt while I looked out the car window at a mountain
(Emigrant Peak). We need girls and mountains frequently.

If I can clean up my brain, perhaps a stick of dynamite will
be needed, the Sibyl will return as an undiscovered lover.

XXI

He sings from the bottom of a well but she can hear him up
through the oat straw, toads, boards, three entwined snakes.

It quiets the cattle they say mythically as who alive has
tried it, their blank stares, cows digesting song. Rumen.

Her long hissing glides at the roller-skating rink, skates
to calves to thighs to ass in blue satin and organ music.

How could you be sane if 250,000 came to the Isle of Wight
to hear your songs near the sea and they looked like an ocean?

Darling companion. We'll listen until it threatens and walls
fall to trumpet sounds or not and this true drug lifts us up.

That noise that came to us out in the dark, grizzly, leviathan,
drags the dead horse away to hollow swelling growls.

XXII

Maps. Maps. Maps. Venezuela, Keewanaw, Iceland open up
unfolding and when I get to them they'll look like maps.

New pilgrims everywhere won't visit tombs, need living
monuments to live again. But there are only tombs to visit.

They left her in the rain tied to the water with cobwebs,
stars stuck like burrs to her hair. I found her by her wailing.

It's obvious I'll never go to Petersburg and Akhmadulina
has married another in scorn of my worship of her picture.

You're not fooling yourself – if you weren't a coward you'd be
another target in Chicago, tremulous bull's-eye for hog fever.

XXIII

I imagined her dead, killed by some local maniac who
crept upon the house with snowmobile at low throttle.

Alcohol that lets me play out hates and loves and fights;
in each bottle is a woman, the betrayer and the slain.

I insist on a one-to-one relationship with nature.
If Thursday I'm a frog it will have to be my business.

You are well. You grow taller. Friends think I've bought you
stilts but it is I shrinking, up past my knees in marl.

She said take out the garbage. I trot through a field with the
sack in my teeth. At the dump I pause to snarl at a rat.

XXIV

This amber light floating strangely upward in the woods – nearly
dark now with a warlock hooting through the tips of trees.

If I were to be murdered here as an Enemy of the State you would
have to bury me under that woodpile for want of a shovel.

She was near the window and beyond her breasts I could see
the burdock, nettles, goldenrod in a field beyond the orchard.

We'll have to abandon this place and live out of the car again.
You'll nurse the baby while we're stuck in the snow out of gas.

The ice had entered the wood. It was twenty below and the beech
easy to split. I lived in a lean-to covered with deerskins.

I have been emptied of poison and returned home dried
out with a dirty bill of health and screaming for new wine.

XXV

O happy day! Said *overpowered,* had by it all and transfixed
and unforgetting other times that refused to swirl and flow.

The calendar above my head made of unnatural numbers, day
lasted five days and I expect a splendid year's worth of dawn.

Rain pumps. Juliet in her tower and Gaspara Stampa again and
that girl lolling in the hammock with a fruit smell about her.

Under tag alder, beneath the ferns, crawling to know animals
for hours, how it looks to them down in this lightless place.

The girl out in the snows in the Laurentians saves her money
for Montreal and I am to meet her in a few years by "accident."

Magdalen comes in a waking dream and refuses to cover me,
crying out for ice, release from time, for a cool spring.

XXVI

What will I do with seven billion cubic feet of clouds
in my head? I want to be wise and dispense it for quarters.

All these push-ups are making me a muscular fatman. Love would
make me lean and burning. Love. Sorry the elevator's full.

She was zeroed in on by creeps and forgot my meaningful glances
from the door. But then I'm walleyed and wear used capes.

She was built entirely of makeup, greasepaint all the way through
like a billiard ball is a billiard ball beneath its hard skin.

We'll have to leave this place in favor of where the sun
is cold when seen at all, bones rust, it rains all day.

The cat is mine and so is the dog. You take the orchard,
house and car and parents. I'm going to Greenland at dawn.

XXVII

I want a sign, a heraldic bird, or even an angel at midnight
or a plane ticket to Alexandria, a room full of good dreams.

This won't do; farmlife with chickens clucking in the barnyard,
lambs, cows, vicious horses kicking when I bite their necks.

The woman carved of ice was commissioned by certain unknown
parties and lasted into a March thaw, tits turning to water.

Phone call. That strange cowboy who pinned a button to the boy's
fly near the jukebox – well last night he shot his mom.

Arrested, taken in as it were for having a purple fundament,
a brain full of grotesqueries, a mouth exploding with red lies.

Hops a plane to NYC riding on the wing through a thunderstorm,
a parade, a suite at the Plaza, a new silver-plated revolver.

XXVIII

In the hotel room (far above the city) I said I bet you
can't crawl around the room like a dog hoho. But she could!

All our cities are lewd and slippery, most of all San Francisco
where people fuck in the fog wearing coarse wool.

And in Los Angeles the dry heat makes women burn so that
lubricants are fired in large doses from machine guns.

We'll settle the city question by walking deeply into forests
and in reasonably vestal groves eat animal meat and love.

I'm afraid nothing can be helped and all letters must be
returned unopened. Poetry must die so poems will live again.

Mines: there were no cities of golden-haired women down there
but rats, raccoon bones, snake skeletons and dark. Black dark.

XXIX

For my horse, Brotherinlaw, who had no character
breaking into panic at first grizzly scent.

Stuff this up your ass New York City you hissing
clip joint and plaster-mouthed child killer.

In Washington they eat bean soup and there's
bean soup on the streets and in the mouths of monuments.

The bull in the grove of lodgepole pines, a champion
broke his prick against a cow and is now worthless.

For that woman whose mouth has paper burns
a fresh trout, salt, honey, and healing music.

XXX

I am walked on a leash by my dog and am water
only to be crossed by a bridge. Dog and bridge.

An ear not owned by a face, an egg without a yolk
and my mother without a rooster. Not to have been.

London has no bees and it is bee time. No hounds
in the orchard, no small craft warnings or sailing ships.

In how many poems through how many innocent branches
has the moon peeked without being round.

This song is for New York City who peeled me like
an apple, the fat off the lamb, raw and coreless.

XXXI

I couldn't walk across that bridge in Hannibal
at night. I was carried in a Nash Ambassador.

On Gough Street the cars went overhead. I counted
two thousand or more one night before I slept.

She hit him in the face with her high-heeled shoe
as he scrambled around the floor getting away.

What am I going to do about the mist and the canning
factory in San Jose where I loaded green beans all night?

Billions of green beans in the Hanging Gardens off Green
Street falling softly on our heads, the dread dope again.

XXXII

All those girls dead in the war from misplaced or aimed
bombs, or victims of the conquerors, some eventually happy.

My friends, he said after midnight, you all live badly.
Dog's teeth grew longer and wife in bed became a lizard.

Goddamn the dark and its shrill violet hysteria.
I want to be finally sane and bow to all sentient creatures.

I'll name all the things I know new and old any you may
select from the list and remember the list but forget me.

It was cold and windy and the moon blew white fish across
the surface where phosphorescent tarpon swam below.

Ice in the air and the man just around the corner has a gun
and that nurse threw a tumor at you from the hospital window.

XXXIII

That her left foot is smaller if only slightly
than her right and when bare cloven down to the arch.

Lovers when they are up and down and think they are whirling
look like a pink tractor tire from the ceiling.

Drag the wooden girl to the fire but don't throw
her in as would the Great Diana of Asia.

Oh the price, the price price. Oh the toll, the toll toll.
Oh the cost, the cost cost. Of her he thought.

To dogs and fire, Bengal tiger, gorilla, Miura bull
throw those who hate thee, let my love be perfect.

I will lift her up out of Montana where her hoof
bruised my thigh. I planted apple trees all day.

XXXIV

When she walked on her hands and knees in the Arab
chamber the fly rod, flies, the river became extinct.

When I fall out of the sky upon you again I'll
feather at the last moment and come in feet first.

There are rotted apples in the clover beneath the fog
and mice invisibly beneath the apples eat them.

There is not enough music. The modal chord I carried
around for weeks is lost for want of an instrument.

In the eye of the turtle and the goldfish and the dog
I see myself upside down clawing the floor.

XXXV

When she dried herself on the dock a drop of water
followed gravity to her secret place with its time lock.

I've been sacrificed to, given up for, had flowers
left on my pillow by unknown hands. The last is a lie.

How could she cheat on me with that African? Let's refer
back to the lore of the locker room & shabby albino secrets.

O the shame of another's wife especially a friend's.
Even a peek is criminal. That greener grass is brown.

Your love for me lasted no longer than my savings for Yurp.
I couldn't bear all those photos of McQueen on your dresser.

Love strikes me any time. The druggist's daughter, the 4-H
girl riding her blue-ribbon horse at canter at the fair.

XXXVI

A scenario: I'm the Star, Lauren, Faye, Ali, little stars,
we tour America in a '59 Dodge, they read my smoldering poems.

I climbed the chute and lowered myself onto the Brahma bull,
we jump the fence trampling crowds, ford rivers, are happy.

All fantasies of a life of love and laughter where I hold your
hand and watch suffering take the very first boat out of port.

The child lost his only quarter at the fair but under the grandstand
he finds a tunnel where all cowshit goes when it dies.

His epitaph: he could dive to the bottom or he paddled in black
water or bruised by flotsam he drowned in his own watery sign.

In the morning the sky was red as were his eyes and his brain
and he rolled over in the grass soaked with dew and said no.

XXXVII

Who could knock at this door left open, repeat
this after me and fold it over as an endless sheet.

I love or I am a pig which perhaps I should be,
a poisoned ham in the dining room of Congress.

Not to kill but to infect with mercy. You are known
finally by what magazines you read in whose toilet.

I'll never be a cocksman or even a butterfly. The one
because I am the other, and the other, the other one.

This is the one song sung loud though in code: I love.
A lunepig shot with fatal poison, butterfly, no one.

XXXVIII

Once and for all to hear, I'm not going to shoot anybody
for any revolution. I'm told it hurts terribly to be shot.

Think that there are miniature pools of whiskey in your flesh
and small deposits of drugs and nicotine encysted in fat.

Beautiful enchanted women (or girls). Would you take your
places by my side, or do you want to fuck up your lives elsewhere?

The veteran said it was "wall-to-wall death" as the men had
been eating lunch, the mortar had hit, the shack blown to pieces.

We'll pick the first violets and mushrooms together & loiter
idyllically in the woods. I'll grow goat feet & prance around.

Master, master, he says, where can I find a house & living
for my family, without blowing my whole life on nonsense?

XXXIX

If you laid out all the limbs from the Civil War hospital
in Washington they would encircle the White House seven times.

Alaska cost two cents per acre net and when Seward
slept lightly he talked to his wife about ice.

My heart is Grant's for his bottle a day and his
foul mouth, his wife that weighed over five hundred pounds.

A hundred years later Walt Whitman often still
walks the length of the Potomac and *on* the water.

A child now sees it as a place for funerals and bags
of components beneath the senators' heads.

XL

If you were less of a vowel or had a full stop in your
brain. A cat's toy, a mouse stuffed with cotton.

It seems we must reject the ovoid for the sphere,
the sphere for the box, the box for the eye of the needle.

And the world for the senate for the circus
for the war for a fair for a carnival. The hobbyhorse.

The attic for a drawer and the drawer for a shell.
The shell for the final arena of water.

That fish with teeth longer than its body is ours
and the giant squid who scars the whale with sucker marks.

XLI

Song for Nat King Cole and the dog who ate the baby
from the carriage as if the carriage were a bowl.

A leafy peace & wormless earth we want, no wires,
connections, struts or props, only guitars and flutes.

The song of a man with a dirty-minded wife – there is
smoke from her pit which is the pit of a peach.

I wrenched my back horribly chopping down a tree – quiff,
quim, queeritus, peter hoister, pray for torn backs.

The crickets are chirping tonight and an ant crosses
the sleeping body of a snake to get to the other side.

I love the inventions of men, the pea sheller, the cherry
picker, the hay baler, the gun and throne and grenade.

XLII

New music might, that sucks men down in howls
at sea, please us if trapped in the inner ear.

When rising I knew there was a cock in that dream
where it shouldn't have been I confess I confess.

Say there this elbow tips glass upward, heat rolls
down in burns, say hallow this life hid under liquid.

Late in the morning Jesus ate his second breakfast,
walked out at five years, drove his first nail into a tree.

Say the monkey's jaw torn open by howling, say after
the drowned man's discovered scowling under the harbor's ice.

XLIII

Ghazal in fear there might not be another
to talk into fine white ash after another blooms.

He dies from it over and over; Duncan has
his own earth to walk through. Let us borrow it.

Mary is Spanish and from her heart comes forth
a pietà of withered leather, all bawling bulls.

Stand in the wine of it, the clear cool gold
of this morning and let your lips open now.

The fish on the beach that the blackbirds eat
smell from here as dead men might after war.

XLIV

That's a dark trough we'd hide in. Said his
sleep without *frisson* in a meadow beyond Jupiter.

It is no baronet of earth to stretch to – flags
planted will be only flags where no wind is.

Hang me rather there or the prez's jowl on a stick
when we piss on the moon as a wolf does NNW of Kobuk.

I'll be south on the Bitterroot while you're up there
and when you land I'll fire a solitary shot at moonface.

I wish you ill's ills, a heavy thumb & slow hands
and may you strike hard enough to see nothing at all.

XLV

What in coils works with riddle's logic, Riemann's
time a cluster of grapes moved and moving, convolute?

As nothing is separate from Empire the signs change
and move, now drawn outward, not "about" but "in."

The stars were only stars. If I looked up then it was
to see my nose flaring on another's face.

Ouspensky says, from one corner the mind looking for
herself may go to another then another as I went.

And in literal void, dazzling dark, who takes
who where? We are happened upon and are found at home.

XLVI

O she buzzed in my ear "I love you" and I dug at
the tickle with a forefinger with which I *knew* her.

At the post office I was given the official FBI
Eldridge Cleaver poster – "Guess he ain't around here."

The escaping turkey vulture vomits his load of rotten
fawn for quick flight. The lesson is obvious & literary.

We are not going to rise again. Simple as that.
We are not going to rise again. Simple as that.

I say it from marrow depth I miss my tomcat gone now from
us three months. He was a fellow creature and I loved him.

XLVII

The clouds swirling low past the house and
beneath the treetops and upstairs windows, tin thunder.

On the hill you can see far out at sea a black ship
burying seven hundred yards of public grief.

The fish that swam this morning in the river swims
through the rain in the orchard over the tips of grass.

Spec. Forces Sgt. Clyde Smith says those fucking
vc won't come out in the open and fight. O.K. Corral.

This brain has an abscess which drinks whiskey
turning the blood white and milky and thin.

The white dog with three legs dug a deep
hole near the pear tree and hid herself.

XLVIII

Dog, the lightning frightened us, dark house and both of us
silvered by it. Now we'll have three months of wind and cold.

Safe. From miracles and clouds, cut off from you and your
earthly city, parades of rats, froth, and skull tympanums.

The breathing in the thicket behind the beech tree was a deer
that hadn't heard me, a doe. I had hoped for a pretty girl.

Flickers gathering, swallows already gone. I'm going south
to the Yucatán or Costa Rica and foment foment and fish.

In the Sudan grass waving, roots white cords, utterly hidden
and only the hounds could find me assuming someone would look.

The sun shines coldly. I aim my shotgun at a ship at sea
and say nothing. The dog barks at the ship and countless waves.

XLIX

After the "invitation" by the preacher she collapsed in the
aisle and swallowed her tongue. It came back out when pried.

No fire falls and the world is wet not to speak of gray and
heat resistant. This winter the snow will stay forever.

The dead cherry trees diseased with leaf rot were piled and
soaked with fuel oil, flames shooting upward into the rain.

Rouse your soul to frenzy said Pasternak. Icons built
of flesh with enough heat to save a life from water.

A new sign won't be given and the old ones you forgot won't
return again until the moment before you die, unneeded then.

Fuse is wet, match won't light it and nothing will. Heat comes
out of the center, radiates faintly and no paper will burn.

L

A boot called Botte Sauvage renders rattlers harmless but they
cost too much; the poet bitten to death for want of boots.

I'm told that black corduroy offers protection from moonburn
and that if you rub yourself with a skunk, women will stay away.

There is a hiding place among the relics of the fifties, poets
hiding in the trunks of Hudson Hornets off the Merritt Parkway.

They said she was in Rome with her husband, a sculptor, but
I'm not fooled. At the Excelsior I'll expose her as a whore.

Down in the canyon the survivors were wailing in the overturned
car but it was dark, the cliffs steep, so we drove on to the bar.

She wants affection but is dressed in aluminum siding and her
edges are jagged; when cold, the skin peels off the tongue at touch.

LI

Who could put anything together that would stay in one place
as remorseless as that cabin hidden in the maple grove.

In Nevada the whores are less clean and fresh than in
Montana, and do not grow more beautiful with use.

The car went only seventeen miles before the motor burned up
and I sat in the grass thinking I had been taken and was sad.

This toothache means my body is wearing out, new monkey glands
for ears in the future, dog teeth, a pink transplanted body.

She is growing old. Of course with the peach, apple, plum,
you can eat around the bruised parts but still the core is black.

Windemere and Derwent Water are exhausted with their own
charm and want everyone to go back to their snot-nosed slums.

LII

I was lucky enough to have invented a liquid heart
by drinking a full gallon of DNA stolen from a lab.

To discover eleven more dollars than you thought you
had and the wild freedom in the tavern that follows.

He's writing mood music for the dead again and ought to have
his ass kicked though it is bruised too much already by his sport.

Both serpent becoming dragon and the twelve moons lost
at sea, worshiped items, rifts no longer needed by us.

Hot Mickey Mouse jazz and the mice jigging up the path
to the beehive castle, all with the bleached faces of congressmen.

LIII

These corners that stick out and catch on things
and I don't fill my body's clothes.

Euclid, walking in switchbacks, kite's tip, always
either *up* or *down* or both, triangular tongue & cunt.

Backing up to the rose tree to perceive which of its
points touch where. I'll soon be rid of you.

There are no small people who hitch rides on snakes
or ancient people with signs. I am here now.

That I will be suicided by myself or that lids close over
and over simply because they once were open.

We'll ask you to leave this room and brick up the door
and all the doors in the hallway until you go outside.

LIV

Aieeee was said in a blip the size of an ostrich egg,
blood pressures to a faint, humming heart flutters.

I can't die in this theater – the movie, *Point Blank,*
god's cheap abuse of irony. But the picture is fading.

This dry and yellow heat where each chicken's
scratch uproots a cloud and hay bursts into flame.

The horse is enraged with flies and rolls over
in the red dirt until he is a giant liver.

From the mailman's undulant car and through the lilacs
the baseball game. The kitchen window is white with noon.

LV

The child crawls in widening circles, backs to the wall
as a dog would. The lights grow dim, his mother talks.

Swag: a hot night and the clouds running low were brains and I
above them with the moon saw down through a glass skull.

And O god I think I want to sleep within some tree
or on a warmer planet beneath a march of asteroids.

He saw the lady in the Empire dress raise it to sit bare
along the black tree branch where she sang a ditty of nature.

They are packing up in the lamplight, moving out again
for the West this time sure only of inevitable miracles.

No mail delights me as much as this – written with plum juice
on red paper and announcing the rebirth of three dead species.

LVI

God I am cold and want to go to sleep for a long time
and only wake up when the sun shines and dogs laugh.

I passed away in my sleep from general grief and a seven-
year hangover. Fat angels wrapped me in traditional mauve.

A local indian maiden of sixteen told the judge to go
fuck himself, got thirty days, died of appendicitis in jail.

I molded all the hashish to look like deer & rabbit turds
and spread them in the woods for rest stops when I walk.

Please consider the case closed. Otis Redding died in a
firestorm and we want to put him together again somehow.

LVII

I thought it was night but found out the windows were painted
black and a bluebird bigger than a child's head was singing.

When we get out of Nam the pilot said we'll go down to S.A.
and kick the shit outta those commie greasers. Of course.

In sleepwalking all year long I grew cataracts, white-haired,
flesh fattened, texture of mushrooms, whistled notes at moon.

After seven hours of television and a quart of vodka he wept
over the National Anthem. O America Carcinoma the eagle dead.

Celebrate her with psalms and new songs – she'll be fifteen
tomorrow, a classic beauty who won't trouble her mind with poems.

I wanted to drag a few words out of silence then sleep and none
were what I truly wanted. So much silence and so many words.

LVIII

These losses are final – you walked out of the grape arbor
and are never to be seen again and you aren't aware of it.

I set off after the grail seven years ago but like a spiral
from above these circles narrow, tighten into a single point.

Let's forgive her for her Chinese-checker brain and the pills
that charge it electrically. She's pulled the switch too often.

After the country dance in the yellow Buick Dynaflow with
leather seats we thought Ferlin Husky was singing to us.

A bottle of Corbys won you. A decade later on hearing
I was a poet you laughed. You are permanently coarsened.

Catherine near the lake is a tale I'm telling – a whiff
of lilac and a girl bleeds through her eyes like a pigeon.

LIX

On the fourteenth Sunday after Pentecost I rose early
and went fishing where I saw an osprey eat a bass in a tree.

We are not all guilty for anything. Let all stupefied
Calvinists take pleasure in sweet dirty pictures and gin.

As an active farmer I'm concerned. Apollinaire fertilizer
won't feed the pigs or chickens. Year of my seventh failure.

When we awoke the music was faint and a golden light came
through the window, one fly buzzed, she whispered another's name.

Let me announce I'm not against homosexuality. Now that the air
is clear on this issue you can talk freely Donny Darkeyes.

A home with a heated garage where dad can tinker with his
poetry on a workbench and mom glazes the steamed froth for lunch.

LX

She called from Sundance, Wyoming, and said the posse had
forced her into obscene acts in the motel. Bob was dead.

The horse kicked the man off his feet and the man rolled
screaming in the dirt. The red-haired girl watched it all.

I've proclaimed June Carter queen-of-song as she makes me
tremble, tears form, chills come. I go to the tavern and drink.

The father ran away and was found near a highway underpass
near Fallon, Nevada, where he looked for shelter from the rain.

My friend the poet is out there in the West being terrified,
he wants to come home and eat well in New York City.

Daddy is dead and late one night won't appear on the porch
in his hunting clothes as I've long wanted him to. He's dead.

LXI

Wondering what this new light is, before he died he walked
across the kitchen and said, "My stomach is very cold."

And this haze, yellowish, covers all this morning, meadow,
orchard, woods. Something bad is happening somewhere to her.

I was ashamed of her Appalachian vulgarity and vaguely askew
teeth, her bad grammar, her wanting to screw more often than I.

It was May wine and the night liquid with dark and fog when
we stopped the car and loved to the sound of frogs in the swamp.

I'm bringing to a stop all my befouled nostalgia about childhood.
My eye was gored out, there was a war and my nickname was *pig*.

There was an old house that smelled of kerosene and apples
and we hugged in a dark attic, not knowing how to continue.

LXII

He climbed the ladder looking over the wall at the party
given for poets by the Prince of China. Fun was had by all.

A certain gracelessness entered his walk and gestures. A tumor
the size of a chickpea grew into a pink balloon in his brain.

I won't die in Paris or Jerusalem as planned but by electrocution
when I climb up the windmill to unscrew the shorted yard lights.

Samadhi. When I slept in the woods I awoke before dawn
and drank brandy and listened to the birds until the moon disappeared.

When she married she turned from a beautiful girl into a
useless sow with mud on her breasts and choruses of oinks.

O the bard is sure he loves the moon. And the inanimate moon
loves him back with silences, and moonbeams made of chalk.

LXIII

O well, it was the night of the terrible jackhammer
and she put my exhausted pelt in the closet for a souvenir.

Baalim. Why can only one in seven be saved from them
and live again? They never come in fire but in perfect cold.

Sepulchral pussy. Annabel Lee of the snows – the night's
too long this time of year to sleep through. Dark edges.

All these songs may be sung to the kazoo and I am not
ashamed, add mongrel's bark, and the music of duck and pig.

Mab has returned as a giantess. She's out there: bombs in
fist and false laurel, dressed antigreen in black metal.

From this vantage point I can only think of you in the
barnyard, one-tenth ounce panties and it's a good vision.

LXIV

That the housefly is guided in flight by a fly brain diminishes
me — there was a time when I didn't own such thoughts.

You admit then you wouldn't love me if I were a dog or rabbit,
was legless with truly bad skin. I have no defense. Same to you.

Poetry (that afternoon, of course) came flying through the
treetops, a shuddering pink bird, beshitting itself in flight.

When we were in love in 1956 I thought I would give up Keats
and be in the UAW and you would spend Friday's check wisely.

Hard rock, acid rock, goofballs, hash, haven't altered my love
for woodcock and grouse. It is the other way around, Mom.

I resigned. Walked down the steps. Got on the Greyhound bus
and went home only to find it wasn't what I remembered at all.

LXV

There was a peculiar faint light from low in the east
and a leaf skein that scattered it on the ground where I lay.

I fell into the hidden mine shaft in Keewanaw, emerging
in a year with teeth and eyes of burnished copper, black skin.

What will become of her, what will become of her now that
she's sold into slavery to an Air Force lieutenant?

I spent the night prophesying to the huge black rock
in the river around which the current boiled and slid.

We'll have to put a stop to this dying everywhere of young
men. It's not working out and they won't come back.

Those poems you wrote won't raise the dead or stir the
living or open the young girl's lips to jubilance.

LETTERS
TO YESENIN

for J.D.

1973

I

to D.G.

This matted and glossy photo of Yesenin
bought at a Leningrad newsstand – permanently
tilted on my desk: he doesn't stare at me
he stares at nothing; the difference between
a plane crash and a noose adds up to nothing.
And what can I do with heroes with my brain fixed
on so few of them? Again nothing. Regard his flat
magazine eyes with my half-cocked own, both
of us seeing nothing. In the vodka was nothing
and Isadora was nothing, the pistol waved
in New York was nothing, and that plank bridge
near your village home in Ryazan covered seven feet
of nothing, the clumsy noose that swung the tilted
body was nothing but a noose, a law of gravity
this seeking for the ground, a few feet of nothing
between shoes and the floor a light-year away.
So this is a song of Yesenin's noose that came
to nothing, but did a good job as we say back home
where there's nothing but snow. But I stood under
your balcony in St. Petersburg, yes St. Petersburg!
a crazed tourist with so much nothing in my heart
it wanted to implode. And I walked down to the Neva
embankment with a fine sleet falling and there was
finally something, a great river vastly flowing, flat
as your eyes; something to marry to my nothing heart
other than the poems you hurled into nothing those
years before the articulate noose.

2

to Rose

I don't have any medals. I feel their lack
of weight on my chest. Years ago I was ambitious.
But now it is clear that nothing will happen.
All those poems that made me soar along a foot
from the ground are not so much forgotten as never
read in the first place. They rolled like moons
of light into a puddle and were drowned. Not even
the puddle can be located now. Yet I am encouraged
by the way you hung yourself, telling me that such
things don't matter. You, the fabulous poet of
Mother Russia. But still, even now, school girls
hold your dead heart, your poems, in their laps
on hot August afternoons by the river while they wait
for their boyfriends to get out of work or their
lovers to return from the army, their dead pets to
return to life again. To be called to supper. You
have a new life on their laps and can scent their
lavender scent, the cloud of hair that falls
over you, feel their feet trailing in the river,
or hidden in a purse walk the Neva again. Best of all
you are used badly like a bouquet of flowers to make
them shed their dresses in apartments. See those
steam pipes running along the ceiling. The rope.

3

I wanted to feel exalted so I picked up
Dr. Zhivago again. But the newspaper was there
with the horrors of the Olympics, those dead and
perpetually martyred sons of David. I want to present
all Israelis with .357 magnums so that they are
never to be martyred again. I wanted to be exalted
so I picked up Dr. Zhivago again but the TV was on
with a movie about the sufferings of convicts in
the early history of Australia. But then the movie
was over and the level of the bourbon bottle was dropping
and I still wanted to be exalted lying there with
the book on my chest. I recalled Moscow but I could
not place dear Yuri, only you Yesenin, seeing the Kremlin
glitter and ripple like Asia. And when drunk you appeared
as some Bakst stage drawing, a slain Tartar. But that is
all ballet. And what a dance you had kicking your legs from
the rope – We all change our minds, Berryman said in Minnesota
halfway down the river. Villon said of the rope that my neck
will feel the weight of my ass. But I wanted to feel exalted
again and read the poems at the end of Dr. Zhivago and
just barely made it. Suicide. Beauty takes my courage
away this cold autumn evening. My year-old daughter's red
robe hangs from the doorknob shouting Stop.

4

I am four years older than you but scarcely an unwobbling
pivot. It was no fun sitting around being famous, was it?
I'll never have to learn that lesson. You find a page torn
out of a book and read it feeling that here you might find
the mystery of print in such phrases as "summer was on the
way" or "Gertrude regarded him somewhat quizzically." Your
Sagane was a fraud. Love poems to girls you never met living
in a country you never visited. I've been everywhere to no
particular purpose. And am well past love but not love poems.
I wanted to fall in love on the coast of Ecuador but the girls
were itsy-bitsy and showers are not prominent in that area.
Unlike Killarney where I also didn't fall in love the girls
had good teeth. As in the movies the Latin girls proved to be
spitfires with an endemic shanker problem. I didn't fall in love
in Palm Beach or Paris. Or London. Or Leningrad. I wanted to fall
in love at the ballet but my seat was too far back to see faces
clearly. At Sadko a pretty girl was sitting with a general
and did not exchange my glance. In Normandy I fell in love but
had colitis and couldn't concentrate. She had a way of not paying
any attention to me that could not be misunderstood. That is
a year's love story. Except Key West where absolutely nothing
happened with romantic overtones. Now you might understand why
I drink and grow fat. When I reach three hundred pounds there
will be no more love problems, only fat problems. Then I will
write reams of love poems. And if she pats my back a cubic yard
of fat will jiggle. Last night I drank a hundred-proof quart
and looked at a photo of my sister. Ten years dead. Show me a
single wound on earth that love has healed. I fed my dying dog
a pound of beef and buried her happy in the barnyard.

5

Lustra. Officially the cold comes from Manitoba;
yesterday at sixty knots. So that the waves mounted
the breakwater. The first snow. The farmers and carpenters
in the tavern with red, windburned faces. I am in there
playing the pinball machine watching all those delicious
lights flutter, the bells ring. I am halfway through
a bottle of vodka and am happy to hear Manitoba
howling outside. Home for dinner I ask my baby daughter
if she loves me but she is too young to talk. She cares
most about eating as I care most about drinking. Our wants
are simple as they say. Still when I wake from my nap
the universe is dissolved in grief again. The baby is sleeping
and I have no one to talk my language. My breath is shallow
and my temples pound. Vodka. Last October in Moscow I taught
a group of East Germans to sing "Fuck Nixon," and we were
quite happy until the bar closed. At the newsstand I saw a
picture of Bella Akhmadulina and wept. Vodka. You would have
liked her verses. The doorman drew near, alarmed. Outside
the KGB floated through the snow like arctic bats.
Maybe I belong there. They won't let me print my verses. On the
night train to Leningrad I will confess everything to someone.
All my books are remaindered and out of print. My face in
the mirror asks me who I am and says I don't know. But stop
this whining. I am alive and a hundred thousand acres of birches
around my house wave in the wind. They are women standing
on their heads. Their leaves on the ground today are small
saucers of snow from which I drink with endless thirst.

6

Fruit and butter. She smelled like the skin of an apple.
The sun was hot and I felt an unbounded sickness with earth.
A single October day began to last a year. You can't fuck
your life away, I thought. But you can! Listening in Nepal
to those peahens scream in the evening. Then, through the glade,
lordly he enters, his ass a ten-foot fan, a painting by a crazed
old master. Look, they are human. Heads the size of two knuckles.
But returning to her buttery appleness and autumn, my dead friend.
We cannot give our lives over to women. Kneeling there under that
vulgar sugar maple tree I couldn't breathe and with a hundred
variations of red above me and against my mouth. She said I'm
going away to Oregon perhaps. I said that I'm going myself to
California where I hear they sleep out every night. So that
ended that and the fan was tucked neatly and the peahens' screams
were heard no more in the land and old ladies and old men slept
soundly again and threw away their cotton earplugs and the earth
of course was soaked with salt and August passed without a single
ear of corn. Of course this was only one neighborhood. Universality
is disgusting. But you had your own truly insurmountable horrors
with that dancer, lacking all wisdom as you did. Your critic said
you were "often revolted by your sensuality." He means
all of that endless fucking of course. Tsk tsk. Put one measure
against another and how rarely they fuse, and how almost never is
there any fire and how often there is only boredom and a craving
for cigarettes, a sandwich, or a drink. Particularly a drink.
I am drunk because I no longer can love. I make love and I'm
writing on a blackboard. Once it was a toteboard, a gun handle
until I myself became a notch. And a notch, to be obvious, is a
nothing. This all must pass as a monk's tale, a future lie.

7

Death thou comest when I had thee least in mind, said Everyman
years ago in England. Can't get around much anymore. So it's
really a terrible surprise unless like you we commit suicide.
I worry some that the rope didn't break your neck, but that
you dangled there strangling from your body's weight. Such
physics can mean a rather important matter of three or four
minutes. Then I would guess there was a moment of black peacefulness
then you were hurtling in space like a mortar. Who can say
if a carcass smiles, if the baggage is happy at full rest. The
child drowns in a predictable puddle or inside the plastic bag
from which you just took your tuxedo. The evening is certainly
ruined and we can go on from there but that too is predictable.
I want to know. I have no explanations for myself but if someone
told me that my sister wasn't with Jesus they would get an
ass-kicking. There's a fascinating tumor called a melanoma
that apparently draws pigment from surrounding tissue until
it's black as coal. That fatal lump of coal tucked against the
spine. And of all things on earth a bullet can hit human
flesh is one of the least resistant. It's late autumn and this
is an official autumnal mood, a fully sanctioned event in which
one may feel the thrill of victory and the agony of defeat. But
as poets we would prefer to have a star fall on us, (that meteor
got me in the gizzard!), or lightning strike us and not while we're
playing golf but perhaps in a wheat field while we're making
love in a thunderstorm, or a tornado take us away outside of
Mingo, Kansas, like Judy Garland unfortunately. Or a rainbow
suffocate us. Or skewered dueling that mighty forces of anti-
art. Maybe in sleep as a Gray Eminence. A painless sleep of course.
Or saving a girl from drowning who turns out to be a mermaid.

8

I cleaned the granary dust off your photo with my shirtsleeve.
Now that we are tidy we can wait for the host to descend
presumably from the sky as that seems to exhaust the alternatives.
You had a nice summer in the granary. I was out there with you
every day in June and July writing one of my six-week wonders,
another novel. Loud country music on the phonograph, wasps
and bees and birds and mice. The horses looked in the window
every hour or so, curious and rather stupid. Chief Joseph stared
down from the wall at both of us, a far nobler man than
we ever thought possible. We can't lead ourselves and he led
a thousand with a thousand horses a thousand miles. He was a god
and had three wives when one is usually more than enough for
a human. These past weeks I have been organizing myself into
my separate pieces. I have the limberness of a man twice my age
and this is as good a time as any to turn around. Joseph was
very understanding, incidentally, when the Cavalry shot so many
of the women and children. It was to be expected. Earth is
full of precedents. They hang around like underground trees
waiting for their chance. The fish swam around four years solid
in preparation for August the seventh, 1972, when I took his life
and ate his body. Just as we may see our own ghosts next to
us whose shapes we will someday flesh out. All of this suffering
to become a ghost. Yours held a rope, manila, straight from
the tropics. But we don't reduce such glories to a mudbath.
The ghost giggles at genuflections. You can't buy him a drink.
Out in a clearing in the woods the other day I got up on a
stump and did a little dance for mine. We know the most fright-
ening time is noon. The evidence says I'm halfway there, such
wealth I can't give away, thirty-four years of seconds.

9

What if I own more paper clips than I'll ever use in this
lifetime? My other possessions are shabby: the house half-
painted, the car without a muffler, one dog with bad eyes
and the other dog a horny moron. Even the baby has a rash on
her neck but then we don't own humans. My good books were
stolen at parties long ago and two of the barn windows are
broken and the furnace is unreliable and field mice daily
feed on the wiring. But the new foal appears healthy though
unmanageable, crawling under the fence and chased by my wife
who is stricken by the flu, not to speak of my own body which
has long suffered the ravages of drink and various nervous
disorders that make me laugh and weep and caress my shotguns.
But paper clips. Rich in paper clips to sort my writings which
fill so many cartons under the bed. When I attach them I say
it's your job after all to keep this whole thing together. And
I used them once with a rubber band to fire holes into the
face of the president hanging on the office wall. We have freedom.
You couldn't do that to Brezhnev much less Stalin on whose
grave Mandelstam sits proudly in the form of the ultimate
crow, a peerless crow, a crow without comparison on earth.
But the paper clips are a small comfort like meeting someone
fatter than myself and we both wordlessly recognize the fact
or meeting someone my age who is more of a drunk, more savaged
and hag-ridden until they are no longer human and seeing
them on the street I wonder how their heads which are only
wounds balance on the top of their bodies. A manuscript of
a novel sits in front of me held together with twenty clips.
It is the paper equivalent of a duck and a company far away
has bought this perhaps beautiful duck and my time is free again.

10

It would surely be known for years after as the day I shot
a cow. Walking out of the house before dawn with the sky an icy
blackness and not one star or cockcrow or shiver of breeze, the rifle
barrel black and icy to the touch. I walked a mile in the dark
and a flushed grouse rose louder than any thunderclap. I entered
a neck of a woodlot I'd scouted and sat on a stump waiting for
a deer I intended to kill. But then I was dressed too warmly
and had a formidable hangover with maybe three hours of sleep so
I slept again seeing a tin open-fronted café in Anconcito down
on the coast of Ecuador and the eyes of a piglet staring at me as
I drank my mineral water dazed with the opium I had taken for
la turista. Crippled syphilitic children begging, one little boy
with a tooth as long as a forefinger, an ivory tusk which would
be pulled on maturity and threaded as an amulet ending up finally
in Moscow in a diplomatic pouch. The boy would explore with his
tongue the gum hole for this Russian gift. What did he know about
Russia. Then carrying a naked girl in the water on my shoulders
and her short hairs tickled the back of my neck with just the suggestion
of a firm grip behind them so if I had been stupid enough to turn
around I might have suffocated at eighteen and not written you
any letters. There were bristles against my neck and hot breath
in my hair. It must be a deer smelling my hair so I wheeled and shot.
But it was a cow and the muzzle blast was blue in the gray light.
She bawled horribly and ran in zigzags. I put her away with a shot
to the head. What will I do with this cow? It's a guernsey and she
won't be milked this morning. I knelt and stared into her huge eyeball,
her iris making a mirror so I combed my hair and thought about the
whole dreary mess. Then I walked backward through a muddy orchard
so I wouldn't be trailed, got in my car and drove to New York nonstop.

II

for Diane W.

No tranquil pills this year wanting to live peeled as they
described the nine throats of Cerberus. Those old greek names
keep popping up. You can tell we went to college and our sleep
is troubled. There are geographical equivalents for exotic tropes
of mind; living peeled was the Desert Inn in Tucson talking with D.W.
about love and art with so much pain my ears rung and the breath
came short. And outside the fine desert air wasn't fine anymore:
the indians became kachina dolls and a girl was tortured daily
for particular reasons. This other is our Akhmatova and often we want
to hide from her – seasoned as she is in so many hells. But why paint
her for one of the dead who knew her pungency of love, the unforgivable
low-tide smell of it, how few of us bear it for long before reducing
it to a civil act. You were odd for a poet attaching yourself
to a woman no less a poet than yourself. It still starts with
the dance. In the end she probably strangled you and maybe back
in Ryazan there was a far better bird with less extravagant plumage.
But to say I'm going to spend the day thinking wisely about
women is to say I'm going to write an indomitably great poem before
lunch or maybe rule the world by tomorrow dawn. And I couldn't
love one of those great SHES – it's far too late and they are far
too few to find anyway though that's a driveling excuse. I saw one
in a tree and on a roof. I saw one in a hammock and thigh-deep
in a pond. I saw one out in the desert and sitting under a willow
by the river. All past tense you notice and past haunting but not
past caring. What did she do to you and did you think of her when
your terrible shadow fell down the wall. I see that creature sitting
on the lawn in Louveciennes, the mistress of a superior secret. We
have both died from want of her, cut off well past our prime.

12

I was proud at four that my father called me Little Turd of Misery.
A special name somehow connected to all the cows and horses in
the perpetual mire of the barnyard. It has a resonance to it un-
known to president senator poet septic-tank cleaner critic butcher
hack or baker liberal or snot, rightist and faker and faggot and
cunt hound. A child was brought forth and he was named Little Turd
of Misery and like you was thrown into the lake to learn how to
swim, owned dogs that died stupidly but without grief. Why does
the dog chase his broken legs in a circle? He almost catches them
like we almost catch our unruly poems. And our fathers and uncles
had ordinary pursuits, hunted and fished, smelled of tobacco and
liquor, grew crops, made sauerkraut and wine, wept in the dark,
chased stray cows, mended fences, were hounded as they say by
creditors. Barns burned. Cabbages rotted. Corn died of drought
before its holy ears were formed, wheat flattened by hail and wind and
the soup grew only one potato and a piece of salt pork from its
center. Generations of slavery. All so we could fuck neurotically
and begin the day rather than end it drinking and dreaming of dead
dogs, swollen creeks with small bridges, ponds where cows are caught
and drown, sucked in by the muck. But the wary boy catches fish
there, steals a chicken for his dog's monthly birthday, learns
to smoke, sees his first dirty picture and sings his first dirty
song, goes away, becomes deaf with song, becomes blinded by love,
gets letters from home but never returns. And his nights become less black
and holy, less moon-blown and sweet. His brain burns away like
gray paraffin. He's tired. His parents are dead or he is dead
to his parents. He smells the smell of a horse. The room is
cold. He dims the light and builds a noose. It works too well.

13

All of those little five-dollar-a-week rooms smelling thick of
cigarette smoke and stale tea bags. The private bar of soap
smearing the dresser top, on the chair a box of cookies and a letter
from home. And what does he think he's doing and do we all begin our
voyage into Egypt this way. The endless bondage of words. That's why
you turned to those hooligan taverns and vodka, Crane to his
sailors in Red Hook. Four walls breathe in and out. The clothes on
the floor are a dirty shroud. The water is stale in its glass.
Just one pull on the bottle starts the morning faster. If you
don't rouse your soul you will surely die while others are having
lunch. Noon. You passed the point of retreat and took that dancer,
a goad, perhaps a goddess. The food got better anyhow and the
bottles. This is all called romantic by some without nostrils
tinctured by cocaine. No romance here, but a willingness to age
and die at the speed of sound. Outside there's a successful revolution
and you've been designated a parasite. Everywhere crushed women
are bearing officious anti-Semites. Stalin begins his diet of
iron shavings and blood. Murder swings with St. Basil's bell, a
thousand per gong free of charge. North on the Baltic Petrodvorets
is empty and inland, Pushkin is empty. Nabokov has sensibly flown
the shabby coop. But a hundred million serfs are free and own
more that the common bread; a red-tinged glory, neither fire nor
sun, a sheen without irony on the land. Who could care that you
wanted to die, that your politics changed daily, that your songs
turned to glass and were broken. No time to marry back in Ryazan,
buy a goat, three dogs, and fish for perch. The age gave you a
pistol and you gave it back, gave you two wives and you gave
them both back, gave you a rope to swing from which you used wisely.
You were good enough to write that last poem in blood.

14

Imagine being a dog and never knowing what you're doing. You're
simply *doing*: eating garbage, fawning, mounting in public with
terrible energy. But let's not be romantic. Those curs, however
sweet, don't have souls. For all of the horrors at least some of
us have better lives than dogs. Show me a dog that ever printed
a book of poems read by no one in particular before he died at
seventeen, old age for a dog. No dog ever equaled Rimbaud for
grace or greatness, for rum running, gun running, slave trading
and buggery. The current phrase, "anything that gets you off,"
includes dogs but they lack our catholicity. Still, Sergei, we never
wanted to be dogs. Maybe indians or princes, Caesars or Mongolian
chieftains, women in expensive undergarments. But if women, lesbians
to satisfy our ordinary tastes for women. In a fantasy if you
become a woman you quickly are caressing your girlfriend. That
pervert. I never thought she would. Be like that. When she's away
from me. Back to consciousness, the room smells like a locker room.
Out the window it's barely May in Moscow and the girls have shed
their winter coats. One watches a group of fishermen. She has
green eyes and is recent from the bath. If you were close enough
which you'll never be you could catch her scent of lemon and
the clear softness of her nape where it meets her hair. She'll
probably die of flu next year or marry an engineer. The same
things really as far as you're concerned. And it's the same in this
country. A fine wife and farm, children, animals, three good reviews.
Then a foggy day in late March with dozens of crows in the air
and a girl on a horse passes you in the woods. Your dog barks.
The girl stops, laughing. She has green eyes. Your heart is off
and running. Your groin hopes. You pray not to see her again.

15

The soul of water. The most involved play. She wonders if she
is permitted to name the stars. Tell her no. This month, May,
is said to be "the month of tiny plant-sucking pests." So even
nature is said to war against us though those pests it seems are
only having lunch. So the old woman had named the stars above
her hut and wondered if god had perhaps given them other names that
she didn't know about. Her priest was always combing his hair
and shining his shoes. We were driven from the church, weren't we
Sergei? In hearses. But is this time for joking? Yes. Always.
We wonder if our fathers in heaven or hell watch when we are about
our lying and shameful acts. As if they up or down there weren't
sick enough of life without watching for eternity some faulty
version of it, no doubt on a kind of TV. Tune the next hour out
dad, I'm going to be bad. Six lines of coke and a moronic twitch.
Please don't watch. I can't help myself. I provide for my children.
They're delighted with the fish I catch. My wife smiles hourly.
She has her horses, dogs, cat, barn, garden. But in New York twenty
layers above the city some cloud or stratum of evil wants to enter
me and I'm certainly willing. Even on ground level in Key West.
Look she has no clothes on and I only wanted to be a friend and
maybe talk about art. Only a lamb. Of course this Little Boy Blue
act is tiresome and believed by no one on earth, heaven or hell.
So we've tried to name the stars and think we are forgiven in
advance. Rimbaud turned to black or arab boys remembering when he
was twelve and there was no evil. Only a helpless sensual wonder.
Pleasure gives. And takes. It is dark and hot and the brain is
howling with those senseless drugs. Mosquitoes land upon those
fields of sweat, the pool between her breasts. You want to be home
rocking your child in a sunny room. Now that it's over. But wait.

16

Today we've moved back to the granary again and I've anointed
the room with *Petrouchka*. Your story, I think. And music. That
ends with you floating far above in St. Petersburg's blue winter
air, shaking your fist among the fish and green horses, the dim-
inuitive yellow sun and chicken playing the bass drum. Your
sawdust is spilled and you are forever borne by air. A simple story.
Another madman, Nijinsky, danced your part and you danced his.
None of us apparently is unique. Think of dying waving a fist full
of ballpoint pens that change into small snakes and that your
skull will be transposed into the cymbal it was always meant to be.
But shall we come down to earth? For years I have been too ready
to come down to earth. A good poet is only a sorcerer bored with
magic who has turned his attention elsewhere. O let us see wonders
that psilocybin never conceived of in her powdery head. Just now
I stepped on a leaf that blew in the door. There was a buzzing
and I thought it concealed a wasp, but the dead wasp turned out to be
a tiny bird, smaller than a hummingbird or june bug. Probably one
of a kind and I can tell no one because it would anger the swarm
of naturalists so vocal these days. I'll tuck the body in my hair
where it will remain forever a secret or tape it to the back of
your picture to give you more depth than any mirror on earth.
And another oddity: the record needle stuck just at the point
the trumpet blast announced the appearance of your ghost in the
form of Petrouchka. I will let it repeat itself a thousand times
through the afternoon until you stand beside the desk in your
costume. But I've no right to bring you back to life. We must
respect your affection for the rope. You knew the exact juncture
in your life when the act of dangling could be made a dance.

17

Behind my back I have returned to life with much more surprise
than conviction. All those months in the cold with neither
tears nor appetite no matter that I was in Nairobi or Arusha, Rome,
the fabled Paris flat and dry as a newsphoto. And lions looked
like lions in books. Only the rumbling sound of an elephant shooting
water into his stomach with a massive trunk made any sense. But I
thought you would have been pleased with the Galla women in Ethiopia
and walking the Colonnade near the Vendôme I knew you had walked
there. Such a few signs of life. Life brings us down to earth he
thinks. Father of two at thirty-five can't seem to earn a living.
But whatever muse there is on earth is not concerned with groceries.
We like to believe that Getty couldn't buy a good line for a billion
dollars. When we first offered ourselves up to her when young and
in our waking dreams she promised nothing. Not certainly that we
could buy a bike for our daughter's birthday or eat good cuts of
beef instead of hamburger. She doesn't seem to care that our wine
is ordinary. She walks in and out the door without knocking. She takes
off her clothes and ruins the marriage bed. She out-and-out killed
you Sergei for no reason I can think of. And you might want to
kill her but she changes so fast whether into a song, a deer, a pig,
the girl sitting on the pier in a short dress. You want to fish
but you turn and there larger than any movie are two thighs and louder
than any howl they beckon you to the life they hold so gently. We
said that her eyes were bees and ice glistened in her hair. And we
know she can become a rope but then you're never sure as all rope
tends to resemble itself though it is common for it to rest in coils
like snakes. Or rope. But I must earn our living and can't think
about rope though I am to be allowed an occasional girl drawing up
her thighs on a pier. You might want her even in your ghostly form.

18

Thus the poet is a beached gypsy, the first porpoise to whom it
occurred to commit suicide. True, my friend, even porpoises have
learned your trick and for similar reasons: losing hundreds of
thousands of wives, sons, daughters, husbands to the tuna nets.
The seventh lover in a row disappears and it can't be endured.
There is some interesting evidence that Joplin was a porpoise and
simply decided to stop breathing at an unknown depth. Perhaps the
navy has her body and is exploring ways to turn it into a weapon.
Off Boca Grande a baby porpoise approached my boat. It was a girl
about the size of my two-year-old daughter who might for all I know
be a porpoise. Anyway she danced around the boat for an hour
while her mother kept a safer distance. I set the mother at ease by
singing my infamous theme song: "Death dupe dear dingle devil flower
bird dung girl," repeating seven times until the mother approached
and I leaned over the gunnel and we kissed. I was tempted to swim
off with them but remembered I had a date with someone who tripled
as a girl, cocaine dealer and duck though she chose to be the last,
alas, that evening. And as in all ancient stories I returned to the
spot but never found her or her little girl again. Even now mariners
passing the spot deep in the night can hear nothing. But enough
of porpoise love. And how they are known to beach themselves. I've
begun to doubt whether we ever would have been friends. Maybe. Not
that it's to the point – I know three one-eyed poets like myself
but am close to none of them. These letters might have kept me
alive – something to do you know as opposed to the nothing you chose.
Loud yeses don't convince. Nietzsche said you were a rope dancer
before you were born. I say yes before breakfast but to the smell
of bacon. Wise souls move through the dark only one step at a time.

19

Naturally we would prefer seven epiphanies a day and an earth
not so apparently devoid of angels. We become very tired with
pretending we like to earn a living, with the ordinary objects and
events of our lives. What a beautiful toothbrush. How wonderful
to work overtime. What a nice cold we have to go with the cold
crabbed spring. How fun to have no money at all. This thin soup
tastes great. I'm learning something every morning from cheap wine
hangovers. These rejection slips are making me a bigger person.
The mailbox is always so empty let's paint it pink. It's good for
my soul that she prefers to screw another. Our cat's right eyeball
became ulcerated and had to be pulled but she's the same old cat.
I can't pay my taxes and will be sent to prison but it will probably
be a good experience. That rattlesnake striking at dog and daughter
was interesting. How it writhed beautifully with its head cut
off and dog and daughter were tugging at it. How purging to lose
our last twenty dollars in a crap game. Seven come eleven indeed.
But what grand songs you made out of an awful life though you had
no faith that less was more, that there was some golden splendor
in humiliation. After all those poems you were declared a coward
and a parasite. Mayakovsky hissed in public over your corpse and
work only to take his own life a little while later. Meanwhile
back in America Crane had his Guggenheim year and technically jumped
ship. Had he been seven hundred feet tall he would have been OK.
I suspect you would have been the kind of friends you both needed
so badly. So many husbands have little time for their homosexual
friends. But we should never imagine we love this daily plate of shit.
The horses in the yard bite and chase each other. I'll make a carol
of my dream: carried in a litter by lovely women, a 20 lb. bag of cocaine,
angels shedding tunics in my path, all dead friends come to life again.

20

The mushrooms helped again: walking hangdoggedly to the granary
after the empty mailbox trip I saw across the barnyard at the base
of an elm stump a hundred feet away a group of white morels. How
many there were will be kept concealed for obvious reasons. While
I plucked them I considered each a letter from the outside world
to my little cul-de-sac, this valley: catching myself in this act
doing what I most despise, throwing myself in the laps of others.
Save my life. Help me. By return post. That sort of thing. So we
throw ourselves in the laps of others until certain famous laps
grow tired, vigorous laps whose movement is slowed by the freight
of all those cries. Then if you become famous after getting off
so many laps you can look at the beautiful women at your feet and
say I'll take that foot and that breast and that thigh and those lips
you have become so denatured and particular. They float and merge
their parts trying to come up with something that will please you.
Selecting the finest belly you write your name with a long thin
line of cocaine but she is perspiring and you can't properly snort
it off. Disappointments. The belly weeps but you dismiss her, sad
and frightened that your dreams have come to no end. Why cast Robert
Redford in your life story if all that he's going to do is sit there
and piss and moan at the typewriter for two hours in expensive
Eastman color? Not much will happen if you don't like to drink
champagne out of shoes. And sated with a half-dozen French meals a day
you long for those simple boiled potatoes your estranged wife made
so perfectly. The letters from your children are defiled in a stack
of fan mail and obscene photos. Your old dog and horse have been
given to kindly people and your wife will soon marry a jolly farmer.
No matter that your million-selling books are cast in bronze. On a
whim you fly to Palm Beach, jump on your yacht and set the automatic.
You fit a nylon hawser around your neck, hurl overboard, and after
the sharks have lunch your head skips in the noose like a marlin bait.

21

To answer some of the questions you might ask were you alive and
had we become friends but what do poets ask one another after long
absence? How have you been other than dead and how have I been
dying on earth without naming the average string of complaints which
is only worrying aloud, naming the dreaded motes that float around
the brain, those pink balloons calling themselves poverty, failure,
sickness, lust, and envy. To mention a very few. But you want part-
iculars, not the human condition or a letter to the editor on why
when I'm at my worst I think I've been fucked over. So here's this
Spring's news: now that the grass is taller I walk in some fear of
snakes. Feeling melancholy I watched my wife plant the garden row
on row while the baby tried to catch frogs. It's hard not to eat too
much when you deeply love food but I've limited myself to a half
gallon of Burgundy a day. On long walks my eyes are so sunk back
in my brain they see nothing, then move forward again toward the light
and see a high meadow turning pale green and swimming in the fog
with crows tracing perceptible and geometrical paths just above
the fog but audible. At the shore I cast for fish, some of them
large with deliquescing smelt and alewives in their bellies. Other
than marriage I haven't been in love for years; close calls over
the world I mentioned to you before, but it's not love if it isn't
a surprise. I look at women and know deeply they are from another
planet and sometimes even lightly touching a girl's arm I know
I am touching a lovely though alien creature. We don't get back
those days we don't caress, don't make love. If I could get you out
in the backcountry down in Key West and get some psilocybin into
you you would cut your legendary vodka consumption. Naturally I
still believe in miracles and the holy fate of the imagination. How
is it being dead and would I like it and should I put it off for a while?

22

These last few notes to you have been a bit somber like biographies
of artists written by joyless people so that the whole book is
a record of agony at thirty rather than thirty-three and a third.
You know the sound – Keeeaaattts wuzzz verrry unhappppppy abouttt
dyinnnng. So here are some of those off-the-wall extravagancies.
Dawn in Ecuador with mariachi music, dawn at Ngorongoro with elephant
far below in the crater swaggering through the marsh grass, dawn in
Moscow and snowing with gold minarets shouting that you have at last
reached Asia, dawn in Addis Ababa with a Muslim waver in the cool
air smelling of ginger and a lion roaring on the lawn, dawn in
bleary Paris with a roll tasting like zinc and a girl in a cellophane
blouse staring at you with four miraculous eyes, dawn in Normandy
with a conceivable princess breathing in the next room and horses
wandering across the moat beneath my window, dawn in Montana with
herons calling from the swamp, dawn in Key West wondering if it was
a woman or tarpon that left your bed before cockcrow, dawn at home
when your eyes are molten and the ghost of your dog chases the fox
across the pasture, dawn on the Escanaba with trout dimpling the
mist and the water with a dulcet roar, dawn in London when the party-
girl leaves your taxi to go home to Shakespeare, dawn in Leningrad
with the last linden leaves falling and you knocking at the door
for a drunken talk but I am asleep. Not to speak of the endless and
nearly unconscious water walks after midnight when even the stars
might descend another foot to get closer to earth. Heat. The wetness
of air. Couplings. Even the mosquitoes are lovely and seem to imitate
miniature birds. And a lion's cough is followed rhythmically by a
hyena's laugh to prove that nature loves symmetry. The black girl
leaves the grand hotel for her implausibly shabby home. The poet
had dropped five sorts of drugs in his belly swill of alcohol and
has imagined his deathless lines commemorating your last Leningrad night.

23

I want to bother you with some recent nonsense; a classmate dropped
dead, his heart was attacked at thirty-three. At the crematory
they lowered his body by fire-resistant titanium cables reminding
one of the steak on a neglected barbecue grill, only more so. We're
not supposed to believe that the vase of ashes is the real him.
You can imagine the mighty roar of the gas jets, a train coming
closer, the soul of thunder. But this is only old hat, or old death,
whichever. "Pause here, son of sorrow, remember death," someone once
said. "We can't have all things here to please us, our little Sue Ann
is gone to Jesus," reads an Alabama gravestone. But maybe even Robert
Frost or Charles Olson don't know they are dead. That would include
you of course. It is no quantity, absolute zero, the air in a hole
minus its airiness, the vacuum from the passing bird or bullet, the
end of the stem where the peach was, the place above the ground
where the barn burned with such energy we plugged our ears. If not,
show yourself in ten minutes. Let's settle this issue because I feel
badly today: a sense that my teeth and body are rotting on the hoof.
I could avoid the whole thing with a few drinks – it's been over
eight hours – but I want to face it like Simon Magus or poor Faustus.
Nothing, however, presents itself other than that fading picture of
my sister with an engine in her lap, not a very encouraging item
to be sure. I took Anna who is two for her first swim today. We didn't
know we were going swimming so she wore a pink dress, standing in
the lake up to her waist in wonderment. The gaucheries of children,
the way they love birds and neon lights, kill snakes and eat sand.
But I decided I wanted to go swimming for the first time and wanted
to make love for the first time again. These thoughts can make you
unhappy. Perhaps if your old dog had been in the apartment that night
you wouldn't have done it. Everything's so fragile except ropes.

24

Dear friend. It rained long and hard after a hot week and when I
awoke the world was green and leafy again, or as J.D. says, everything
was new like a warm rain after a movie. And I said enough of death
and its obvious health hazards, it's a white-on-white jigsaw puzzle
in one piece. An hour with the doctor yesterday when he said my
blood pressure was so high I might explode as if I had just swallowed
an especially tasty grenade. I must warn my friends not to stand
too close. Blood can be poisonous; the Kikuyu in Kenya are often
infected when they burrow hacking away in the gut of an elephant.
Some don't come back. But doctors don't say such things, except
W.C. Williams. Just like your doctor when you were going batty, mine
said, "You must be distressed, you eat and drink and smoke far too
much. Cut out these things. The lab found lilacs and part of the
backbone of a garter snake or garter in your stool sample, and the
remnants of a hair ball. Do you chew your comb? We are checking to
see if it's your hair as there are possible criminal questions here.
Meanwhile get this thatch of expensive prescriptions filled and I
advise extensive psychiatric care. I heard your barking when I left
the room. How did you manage gout at your age?" My eyes misted
and I heard fiddle music and I looked up from page 86 in the June
Vogue where my old nemesis Lauren Hutton was staring at me in a
doctor's office in northern Michigan. This is Paul Bunyan country
Lauren. And how did I get gout? All of that fried salt and side
pork as a child. Humble fare. Quintuple heaps of caviar and decanters
of vodka at the Hotel Europa in Leningrad. *Tête de veau*, the brains,
tongue and cheeks of a calf. Side orders of *tripe à la mode de Caen*
sweetbreads with morels. Stewed kidneys and heart. Three-pound steaks
as snacks, five dozen oysters and three lobsters in Boston. A barrel
of nice gravy. Wild boar. Venison. Duck. Partridge. Pig's feet. But
you know, Sergei, I must eat these magical trifles to keep from
getting brainy and sad, to avoid leaving this physical world.

An afterthought to my previous note; we must closely watch any self-pity and whining. It simply isn't manly. Better by far to be a cowboy drinking rusty water, surviving on the maggots that unwittingly ate the pemmican in the saddlebags. I would be the Lone and I don't need no one said the cowpoke. Just a man and his horse against everything else on earth and horses are so dumb they run all day from flies never learning that flies are everywhere. Though in their violent motion they avoid the flies for a few moments. It's time again not to push a metaphor too far. But back again to the successful farmer who has his original hoe bronzed like baby shoes above the Formica mantelpiece – I earned what I got, nobody give me nothing he says. Pasternak said you probably didn't think death was the end of it all. Maybe you were only checking it out for something new to write about. We thieves of fire are capable of such arrogance when not otherwise occupied as real people pretending to be poet farmers, important writers, capable lovers, sports fops, regular guys, rock stars with tiny nonetheless appreciative audiences. But the self-pity and whining must stop. I forgot to add that at the doctor's an old woman called in to say that her legs had turned blue and she couldn't walk or hold her urine and she was alone. Try that one on. Thirty years ago I remember my mother singing *Hello Central, give me heaven, I think my daddy is there* about the usual little boy in a wartime situation. We forget about those actual people, certainly our ancestors and neighbors, who die in earnest. They called my dad, the county agent, and his friend a poor farmer was swinging like you only from a rafter in the barn from a hay rope. What to do with his strange children – their thin bodies, low brows and narrow eyes – who were my schoolmates. They're working in auto factories now and still voiceless. We are different in that we suffer and love, are bored, with our mouths open and must speak on occasion for those others.

26

Going in the bar last Sunday night I noticed that they were having
high-school graduation down the street. Caps and gowns. June and
mayflies fresh from the channel fluttering in the warm still air.
After a few drinks I felt jealous and wanted someone to say, "Best of
luck in your chosen field," or, "The road of life is ahead of you."
Remember your first trip to Moscow at nineteen? Everything was pos-
sible. You watched those noblewomen at the riding academy who would
soon be permanently unhorsed, something you were to have mixed
feelings about, what with the way poets suck up to and are attracted
to the aristocracy however gimcrack. And though the great Blok
welcomed you, you felt tentative, an unknown quantity, and remained
so for several years. But how quickly one goes from being unknown
and embarrassed to bored and arrogant, from being ignored to expecting
deference. From fleabag rooms to at least the Plaza. And the daydreams
and hustling, the fantasies and endless work that get you from one
to the other, only to discover that you really want to go home. Start
over with a new deck. But back home all the animals are dead, the
friends have disappeared and the fields gone to weed. The fish
have flown from the creeks and ponds and the birds have all drowned
or gone to China. No one knows you – they have little time for poetry
in the country, or in the city for that matter except for the minis-
trations of a few friends. Your name bobs up like a Halloween
apple and literature people have the vague feeling that they should read
you if they ever "catch up" on their reading. Once on a train I saw
a girl reading a book of mine but she was homely and I had a toothache
so I let the moment pass. What delicious notoriety. The journalist
said I looked like a bricklayer or beer salesman, not being fashion-
ably slender. But lately the sun shines through, the sweet release
of flinging these lines at the dead, almost like my baby Anna throw-
ing grain to the horses a mile away, in the far corner of the pasture.

27

I won my wings! I got all A's! We bought fresh fruit! The toilet
broke! Thus my life draws fuel ineluctably from triumph. Manic,
rainy June slides into July and I am carefully dressing myself in
primary colors for happiness. When the summer solstice has passed
you know you're finally safe again. That midnight surely dates
the year. "Look to your romantic interests and business investments,"
says the star hack in the newspapers. But what if you have neither?
Millions will be up to nothing. One of those pure empty days with
all the presence of a hole in the ground. The stars have stolen
twenty-four hours and vengeance is out of the question. But I'm
a three-peckered purple goat if you were tied to any planet by your
cord. That is mischief, an inferior magic; pulling the lining out
of a top hat. You merely rolled on the ground moaning trying to pull
that mask off but it had grown into your face. "Such a price the
gods exact for song to become what we sing," said someone. If it
aches that badly you have to take the head off, narrow the neck to
a third its normal size, a practice known as hanging by gift of the
state or as a do-it-yourself project. But what I wonder about is your
velocity: ten years from Ryazan to Leningrad. A little more than
a decade, two years into your fifth seven and on out like a proton
in an accelerator. You simply fell off the edge of the world while
most of us are given circles or, hopefully, spirals. The new
territory had a wall which you went over and on the other side there
was something we weren't permitted to see. Everyone suspects it's
nothing. Time will tell. But how you preyed on, longed for, those
first ten years. We'll have to refuse that, however its freshness
in your hands. Romantic. Fatal. We learn to see with the child's
delight again or perish. We hope it was your vision you lost,
that before those final minutes you didn't find out something new.

28

to Robert Duncan

O to use the word wingéd as in bird or victory or airplane for
the first time. Not for spirit though, yours or anyone else's
or the bird that flew errantly into the car radiator. Or for poems
that sink heavily to our stomachs like fried foods, the powerful
ones, visceral, as impure as the bodies they flaunt. Curious what
you paid for your cocaine to get wingéd. We know the price of
the poems, one body and soul net, one brain already tethered to the
dark, one ingenious leash never to hold a dog, two midwinter eyes
that lost their technicolor. Think what you missed. Mayakovsky's
pistol shot. The Siege of Leningrad. Crows feasting on all of those
frozen German eyes. Good Russian crows that earned a meal putting
up with all of that insufferable racket of war. Curious crows watching
midnight purges, wary of owls, and the girl in the green dress
on the ground before a line of soldiers. She and the crow exchange
pitiless glances. She flaps her arms but is not wingéd. Maybe
there is one ancient crow that remembers the Czarina's jeweled
sleigh, the ring of its small gold bells; and the sickly wingéd
horse in the cellar of the Winter Palace, product of a mad breeding
experiment for eventual escape, how it was dumped into the Neva
before the talons grew through the hooves, the marvel of it lost
in the uproar of those days, the proof of it in the bones somewhere
on the floor of the Baltic delta. But we all get lost in the course
of empire, which lacks the Brownian movement's stability. We count
on iron men to stick to their guns. Our governments are weapons
of exhaustion. Poems fly out of yellow windows at night with a stall
factor just under a foot, beneath our knees and the pre–Fourth of
July corn in the garden. At least at that level radar can't detect
them and they're safe from State interference. We know perfectly
well you flapped your arms madly, unwingéd but craving a little flight.

29

We're nearing the end of this homage that often resembles a
suicide note to a suicide. I didn't mean it that way but how
often our hands sneak up on our throats and catch us unaware.
What are you doing here we say. Don't squeeze so hard. The hands
inside the vodka bottle and on the accelerator, needles and coke-
sore noses. It's not very attractive, is it? But now there is rain
on the tin roof, the world outside is green and leafy with bluebirds
this morning dive-bombing drowning worms from a telephone wire,
the baby laughing as the dog eats the thirty-third snake of the
summer. And the bodies on the streets and beaches. Girl bottoms!
Holy. Tummies in the sun! Very probably holy. Peach evidence almost
struggling for air! A libidinal stew that calls us to life however
ancient and basal. May they plug their lovely ears with their big
toes. God surely loves them to make them look that way and can I
do less than He at least in this respect. As my humble country
father said in our first birds-and-bees talk so many years ago: "That
thing ain't just to pee through." This vulgarity saves us as
certainly as our chauvinism. Just now in midafternoon I wanted
a tumbler of wine but John Calvin said, "You got up at noon. No wine
until you get your work done. You haven't done your exercises to
suppress the gut the newspaper says women find most disgusting.
The fence isn't mended and the neighbor's cow keeps crawling through
in the night, stealing the fresh clover you are saving for Rachel
the mare when she drops her foal." So the wine bottle remains
corked and Calvin slips through the floorboards to the crawl space
where he spends all of his time hating his body. Would these concerns
have saved you? Two daughters and a wife. Children prop our rotting
bodies with cries of *earn earn earn*. On occasion we are kissed. So odd
in a single green month to go from the closest to so far from death.

30

The last and I'm shrinking from the coldness of your spirit: that
chill lurid air that surrounds great Lenin in his tomb as if we
had descended into a cloud to find on the catafalque a man who has
usurped nature, isn't dead any more than you or I are dead. Only
unlikely to meet and talk to our current forms. Today I couldn't
understand words so I scythed ragweed and goldenrod before it could
go to seed and multiply. I played with god imagining how to hold His
obvious scythe that caught you, so unlike the others, aware and
cooperative. Is He glad to help if we're willing? A boring question
since we're so able and ingenious. Sappho's sparrows are always
telling us that love will save us, some *other* will arrive to draw
us cool water, lie down with us in our private darkness and make
us well. I think not. What a fabulous lie. We've disposed of sparrows
and god, the death of color, those who are dominated by noon and
the vision of night flowing in your ears and eyes and down your
throat. But we didn't mean to arrive at conclusions. Fifty years are
only a moment between this granary and a hanged man half the earth
away. You are ten years younger than my grandmother Hulda who still
sings Lutheran hymns and watches the Muskegon River flow. In whatever
we do, we do damage to ourselves; and in those first images there
were always cowboys or cossacks fighting at night, murdered animals
and girls never to be touched; dozing with head on your dog's chest
you understand breath and believe in golden cities where you will
live forever. And that fatal expectancy – not comprehending that we
like our poems are flowers for the void. In those last days you
wondered why they turned their faces. Any common soul knew you
had consented to death, the only possible blasphemy. I write to
you like some half-witted, less courageous brother, unwilling to tease
those ghosts you slept with faithfully until they cast you out.

POSTSCRIPT

At 8:12 AM all of the watches in the world are being wound.
Which is not quite the same thing as all of the guitars on earth
being tuned at midnight. Or that all suicides come after the mail-
man when all hope is gone. Before the mailman, watches are wound,
windows looked through, shoes precisely tied, toothcare, the
attenuations of the hangover noted. Which is not the same as
the new moon after midnight or her bare feet stepping slowly toward
you and the snake easing himself from the ground for a meal.
The world is so necessary. Someone must execute stray dogs and
free the space they're taking up. I can see people walking down
Nevsky Prospect winding their watches before you were discovered
too far above the ground, that mystical space that was somewhere
occupied by a stray dog or a girl in an asylum on her hands
and knees. A hanged face turns slowly from a plum to a lump of
coal. I'm winding my watch in antipathy. I see the cat racing
around the yard in a fantasy of threat. She's preparing for
eventualities. She prizes the only prize. But we aren't the cats
we once were thousands of years ago. You didn't die with the
dignity of an animal. Today you make me want to tie myself to
a tree, stake my feet to earth herself so I can't get away. It didn't
come as a burning bush or pillar of light but I've decided to stay.

A LAST GHAZAL

Anconcito. The fisheater. Men were standing on cork rafts
on the water, visible between great Pacific swells.

So in Ecuador you decide to forget her in St. George in
Normandy. Try not to think of a white horse for several days.

All of the lilacs in the yard lie when they take you back to your
youth. There are white hairs on your chin, you can't jump the fence.

What is this feeling that the police are ineluctably closing
in and you will miss many of your daughters' birthdays.

There are still flowers of evil that want to lead you to another
life. We have photographic evidence of this in color, black-and-white.

Asleep and in a dreaming state near death I feel the awkward girl
in my head say please not now, I haven't quite lived yet.

A DOMESTIC POEM FOR PORTIA

This is all it is.
These pictures cast up in front of me
with the mind's various energies.
Hence so many flies in this old granary.
I've become one of those blackened beef sides
hanging in a South American market so when I sing
to myself I dispel a black cloud around my mouth
and when Linda brings iced tea she thinks I'm only
a photo in the *National Geographic* and drinks the tea
herself, musing he's snuck off to the bar
and his five-year pool game.
This seems to be all it is.
Garcia sings *Brown-eyed women and red grenadine.*
Some mother-source of pleasure so that the guitar
mutes and revolves the vision of her as she rinses
her hair bending thigh-deep in the lake, her buttocks appear
to be struggling by themselves to get out of that bikini
with a faint glisten of sun at each cheek-top.
But when I talked to her she was thin in the head,
a magazine photo slipping through the air like
a stringless kite.
It's apparent now that this is all there is.
This shabby wicker chair, music, the three PM
glass of red wine as a reward for sitting still
as our parents once instructed us. "Sit still!"
I want my head to go visit friends, traveling they call it
and without airports. Then little Anna up to her neck
in the lake for the first time, the ancient lineage
of swimming revealing itself in her two-year-old fat
body, eyes sparkle with awe and delight in this natural
house of water. Hearing a screech I step to the porch

and see three hawks above the neighbor's pasture
chasing each other in battle or courtship.
This must be all there is.
At full rest with female-wet eyes becoming red wondering
falsely how in christ's name am I going to earn
enough to keep us up in the country where the air
is sweet and green, an immense kingdom of water nearby
and five animals looking to me for food, and two daughters
and a mother assuming my strength. I courageously fix
the fence, mulch the tomatoes, fertilize the pasture –
a nickel-plated farmer. Wake up in the middle
of the night frightened, thinking nearly two decades
ago I took my vows and never dreamed I'd be responsible
for so many souls. Eight of them whispering *provide.*
This could very well be all that there is.
And I'm not unhappy with it. A check in the mail that will
take us through another month. I see in the papers
I've earned us "lower class"! How strange. Waiting
for Rachel's foal to drop. That will make nine. Provide.
Count my big belly ten. But there's an odd grace in being
an ordinary artist. A single tradition clipping the heads
off so many centuries. Those two drunks a millennium ago on
a mountaintop in China – laughing over the beauty of the moment.
At peace despite their muddled brains. The male dog, a trifle
stupid, rushes through the door announcing absolutely nothing.
He has great confidence in me. I'm hanging on to nothing today and
with confidence, a sureness that the very air between our bodies,
the light of what we are, has to be enough.

MISSY 1966–1971

I want to be worthy of this waking dream –
    floating   above
    the August landscape
in a coffin with my dog
who's just died from fibroid cancer.
Yes. We'll be up there and absorb
the light of stars and phosphorus
like the new army telescopic sights
and the light hanging captive
in clouds
and the light glittering upward
from the water
and porch lights
from the few trucks & cars
at 3 AM
and one lone airliner.
Grief holding us safe in a knot we'll float
over every mile we covered, birch clump, thorn apple,
wild cherry trees and aspen in search of grouse,
your singular white figure fixed then as Sirius the Dog Star.
I think this crazed boy striking
out at nothing
wants to join you
so homeward
bound.

FOUR MATRICES

1. HOME

New Matrices, all ice. Fixed here and solidly.
What was that song? My grave is hiding from me.
I'll go to that juniper thicket across
the road. Or stay here. Or go. Or stay.
A contessa. A girl on a roan horse behind
the goldenrod. The barn. The whiskey shelf.
Count options, false starts. And glooms of love,
the lover's next-room boredom. Juliet's in Verona.
Juliets are always in Verona after a few days.
Or trout and grouse, wading & walking after them.
Days of it. Dis. Dis. Dis. Dante called it,
this actual hell, this stillness. Lasting
how long? Waking is visionary. I'll awake but
to sleep again, new and bitter each new time.

2. COUNTING ARIZONA

Amphora in rocks. Kachina of fur and rust. The land
here seemed burned out & wasn't; just no lushness
of green, verdigris, leaves in sweet rot or swamps.
I don't belong and won't, perhaps only less foreign
than the natives. INDIANS: Zuni, Navajo, Jicarilla,
Papago, Mescalero Apache, Hopi. Aliens. That range is
owned by cone-nosed beetles, cattle, scorpion and snake
and the mines. A few deer, javelinas, quail, mountain thrush
and jackrabbit. Frightened. I count and point. Beware.
Just off the road's shoulder is wilderness and finally
Mexico and peopleless. And too much sun. I want to go home.

3. HOME

Cores. Knots. A vortex around which nothing swirls
or moves. Here then. Where I am now and can't seem
to move, some perfect cripple; a suspended brain.
It was cold, it is cold. It will be cold. And dry.
A root hits tablerock, curls upward, winds around
itself until it becomes a noose. Obvious! Obvious!
All the better. Simple things: just now a horse walked
past the window. I was naked when I carried the dying dog
to the couch. And weeping with alcohol and rock and
cold and stillness, horses and roots, unmoving brain.

4. THE SEA

Screw-gumption despite cold rain and clouds drifting below treetops.
Poor thing, strung up by false & falser delights; not lost,
a word that weighs nothing except *lost* to one's self, floating.
How light these imagined loves, floating too, from the head
in a night's sleep when the body's heat is nonmental.
It's a happy mage that walks through the world with his eyes
earthward using clouds only for a pick-me-up. The brain's not
a solid thing he thinks eating calf's brains. But butchers
are solid people. Somewhere between butcher and that unstable
weight is ballad, some song, though not moving to our obvious
harmonies. Count those waterbirds and beware, costumed as women;
part air and part water. But we are drawn to them as clumsy
rowboats sunk in fifty fathoms. After drifting the oceans for years.

NORTH AMERICAN IMAGE CYCLE

to Tom McGuane

The boy stood in the burning house. Set it up
that way, and with all windows open. I don't want
a roof. I want to fill all those spaces where we
never allow words to occur.

•••

Crudities:
     implausible as this brilliantly cold
day in late June, barely forty. Two horses outside
the granary door, braced leaning into the wind
not even trying to figure it out.

And the great shattering cold waves
On Good Harbor Bay, the sea permanently bleak;
a squall line a hundred miles long, the island a dull
ugly green, and only one brief sweep of yellow light.

It is nearly against nature and that is why I love
it and would not trade it for all your princely heart.

•••

The snail is beautiful, nearly Persian. Do we dwell *in*
or *on* beauty? The Belgian mare in my barn weighs 2300 lbs.
but thinks of herself oddly as woman, very feminine and shy
tossing her flaxen mane then rolling hugely & wantonly
in the snow. She takes the proffered apple not with her teeth
but delicately with her lips.

···

Phenomenon. Agonies. Mostly unshared. Dear Friends
the nightmare I recounted was pastel. I believed in numbers.
What is so crisp and intense as a number? Not our bodies
in their average frenzies. Fortunately the heart
doesn't melt as wax does at the sight of a kitten.
Place a kitten near a candle when bored.

···

In a dream I saw Spicer's body hanging from a hundred feet
of clothesline rope under the Golden Gate. Ask Weldon Kees
and Lew Welch to make contact, if alive or not. Crane's jump
in all things, a raincoat, borrowed. When I fish the Marquesas
every year I say to the passing fish, have you seen Crane's bones?
How deep and where do they lie and are they drawn together or
spread and are they peaceful on the bottom?

···

Are these horses less wonderful for my daughter having to shovel
horseshit an hour a day? The teacher would say someone has
to do it and go on to the social contract before a lunch of
cheese sandwiches, tomato soup and chalk dust à la mode.
But we are thinking of horses not teachers. And of the shovel
and the dreaded weight at the end that is less useful than
the much ruminated cow manure. Throw it out the door.
Sally, Nancy, Belle, Saud & Tramp watch with soft curious
horse eyes.

···

Oooooooo, he said to himself. That night of wonderment.
The head might explode from it. Certainly the heart beats
in circles like a Masarati cam. The insistence of physical
love and she didn't know her head was in an ashtray and
afterward didn't seem to care.

⋄⋄⋄

More mad dogs and fewer streetlights, Mr. Nixon. That advice
will cost you a hundred bucks, has been billed for that amount.
Date check after the first for tax reasons. The mad
dogs can be gotten from Spain, cheap. And everyone loves
to throw stones at streetlights.

⋄⋄⋄

And my puppy is over her kidney infection, diagnosed
as chronic & fatal. Saved from the gas chamber. I salute
the technology of antibiotics. All dogs are in particular
as was Christopher Smart's cat Jeoffry. He said drunkenly
near dawn O let her sleep with us during her last days and
let her wounds become my own.

⋄⋄⋄

First sighting:
She was up in the apple tree with one leg hanging
and the other drawn under her, sidesaddle on the branch.
Her face was bare of features and being an artist of sorts
I filled them in. It was deadly serious and I wanted
to ask someone what she was doing so nudely up in the apple
tree behind the barn, but had no one to ask and the mouth

I'd designed was too fresh on her face to open; so I stared
up and noticed she didn't lack the truly important features of
her sex but any desire was constrained by fear. So I sat
in the grass and dozed from what I'd been drinking that afternoon
waking to hear her sing no mantra but some ancient lute song,
and seeing her again as she dropped from the tree to my side
I thought her bare feet were cloven a bit too obviously.

•••

At four in the morning my body bumped against the ceiling.
Thank Jesus for ceilings or I would have been lost to earth,
rather, earth lost to me as she doesn't know me well.

•••

Remember her cheers? How you loved the cheerleader far beyond
desperation. How you nearly threw yourself into Niagara Falls
unprotected by a rubber barrel on your high-school senior trip.
Now you have a permanent rubber barrel around you but you
no longer love the cheerleader.

•••

He sang *I'm talking through a hat that isn't mine.* It's
Jackson Pollock's, given him by Pollock's brother, Charles,
and there is blood on the rim, his own not Pollock's. This talisman
was lost in a bar somewhere, anywhere in America, and is
worn now by a dump-picker who found it among the garbage.
Appropriate! As both of them, one so great and the other so
small, treated themselves like garbage. *sanctus detritus redivivus*

•••

237

I felt myself floating toward the shadow of the dreamer I once
was. I said that I had become too old to dream and the androgynous
dreamer said let's marry anyway and be unhappy but joyous
in our dreams. There were poems before books on earth.

•••

The stewardess said You're a poet?
When I think of a poet I think of someone sitting
around all day humming *Got a date with a daydream*.

•••

This fat & sexless life.

•••

I mourned Portia's unfair operation. Then the horse
ate her garden to ground level. The horse's name
happened to be Rex.

•••

We must not think of our country as a ten-trillion-dollar
blowjob no matter how the idea tempts us.

•••

Overheard story in Montana bar: She thought when she lost
her teeth we'd divorce and she cried a lot; so I said
to her we won't divorce but we'll marry someone else. The vaunted
simplicity of cowboys who are really cossacks – the horse
rhythms obviously affecting the brain chemistry. A slavic tribe
with ambivalent affection for guns & ewes, mares & drudgery.

• • •

He became humbler with his journalism, bought a porkpie hat
at Kresge's and wore an inoperable malachite pencil over
his left ear as his only visible rebellion.

• • •

The green green grass of home is owned by another now
and I'm not allowed on the property for my ounce of sentiment.

• • •

In the Montana whorehouse the madam yells "Burma"
through the door to the girl and her customer
when the time is up, circa twenty minutes for twenty
dollars, the value being established by Nixon's Price
Commission on infolding nightflowers, petaled creatures.
So the customer who is a language buff looks down
at his shoes, all that he's wearing, and thinks:
How did I get my pants off over my shoes? Has a genuine
miracle happened? Why do they use Burma as a signal
rather than Peking or Topeka or French fries? On the dresser
is a photo of the girl with a child, her son in a sailor
suit. Does he cry Burma in the night to get his mother
home? A tape cassette playing Wilson Pickett. Can my
future be traced on those stretch marks and if she were
wet would they form small rivers, minnows and all?
That twenty was hard-earned by art to be printed in New York
at $5.95 net. Will she buy him another sailor suit?
The room is hot. Perhaps during the C-minus transport
the house has been moved to Burma and outside is a green

hell with lianas masquerading as vipers and vice versa.
On a tray there is some dental floss, Moon Drop lotion
and a cordless vibrator, an aerosol can of Cupid's Quiver.
I really didn't want to go to Burma this afternoon, ma'am,
he thinks. I'll miss supper and fishing the evening hatch.

••••

Second sighting:
She was up on the roof when I went up to check
the texture of the night and to generally be an ordinary
poet who muses about the Boston skyline from an Alston roof.
She was leaning in the shadows against the none-too-solid
cornice but had no fears of being aerial. Her sex was soft
as a small mound of coal dust, the material
of spiderwebs, a dove's head.

••••

Start with seven for luck:
homo erectus, erect of course,
a compass, viper, wand or club,
gun, usual knife with any her or she
in repose for imagined punishment.
See him shudder, "throb" the books say,
quake, his flanks with a doggish bend.
Her eyes stare past his ear, they are
a green not found in nature and three
feet deep. Nothing need be forgiven.

••••

Awake. A dab of numero uno in the smoking
pipe. The whole table in Montana loves
each other. They are relaxing from a long
day's sleep. The women are beautiful
and clean, the men young and ambitious.
They verge on taking over something not quite
comprehensible. The dance begins. Libidinous.
A horse's nose is pressed against the kitchen
window. It seems the very room wants to rise
up and screw but these are the sons and daughters
of an *entre* act, of Calvin, pre-Korean, middle Nam.
And their eyes are pink with hopeless energy.

    ♦♦♦

He throws a fifty-lire piece in the fountain
and wants to tell his outrageous wish but they
won't listen. The wish won't count if you tell it
she says. He broods. The air is full of these god-
damn wops and their filthy pigeons. What good
is a wish that can't be told, that was wished
to anger those who won't hear it. Give me the single
raindrop that fell through the hole in the pagan
temple as my bride. Wishes must be phrased in old-time
languages, a sort of fatigued Episcopalian; here
and there it wasn't: that pinochle become the national
sport of the U.S.A.; that dysentery disappear straightaway
from earth; that the girl hidden in New York change
her silly predilection for her sisters, fall like
rain through the roof of a pagan temple on this gentle soul.

    ♦♦♦

Grease density

Moon tup

Pink eye

Yellow book

Muddy horse (he fell in the pond)

Great big stomach from reading cookbooks

The child fell

The fly drank then backstroked on the skin of wine then perished

It is a true suntan because her ass is white

Red rock with green lichen

Green ground with red lichen

Since Bob jogs he snores less says his wife

Yes the hoopless barrel will break when filled

We fear the vicious Brazilian honeybee

Her eroticism is fungoid as in fungus

Some of us are aliens from god knows where

The midwest barren without good shellfish

•••

The announcement said get to the high ground
but we were unable to move while the waters
crept up to the window, peeked in, then receded.
There was a fish near the mailbox, a lake trout
with two immature lamprey eels dangling from
their teethhold on the stomach.

•••

For five days the moon was red from the dust storm.
It lost its novelty. Then on the sixth the moon
was pink and regained its novelty. On the seventh

it disappeared though reports from Perth, Australia,
established a white bladder-shaped object in the sky.

•••

Third sighting:
Is she the black-crowned night heron
          our lady of the marshes
hidden at the far end of the lake
the verge of an enormous swamp
hearing her call amid stippled shadow ten thousand tree frogs
          the vision of eros as water bird

emerging from the green brush near midnight
stately wading legs

RETURNING
TO EARTH

for Guy & Anna

What forgotten reverie, what initiation,
it may be, separated wisdom from the
monastery and, creating Merlin,
joined it to passion?

−W.B. Yeats, *A Vision*

1977

RETURNING TO EARTH

She
pulls the sheet of this dance
across me
then runs, staking
the corners far out at sea.

♦♦♦

So curious in the middle of America, the only "locus"
I know, to live and love at great distance. (Growing
up, everyone is willing to drive seventy miles to see
a really big grain elevator, ninety miles for a dance,
two hundred to look over a pair of Belgian mares
returning the next day for the purchase, three hundred
miles to see Hal Newhouser pitch in Detroit, eight
hundred miles to see the Grand Ole Opry, a thousand
miles to take the mongoloid kid to a Georgia faith healer.)
I hitched two thousand for my first glimpse of the Pacific.
When she first saw the Atlantic she said near Key Largo,
"I thought it would be bigger."

♦♦♦

I widowed my small
collection of magic
until it poisoned itself with longing.
I have learned nothing.
I give orders to the rain.
I tried to catch the tempest in a gill net.
The stars seem a little closer lately.
I'm no longer afraid to die
but is this a guidepost of lunacy?

I intend to see the ten hundred million worlds Mañjushri
passed through before he failed to awaken the maiden.
Taking off and landing are the dangerous times.
I was commanded in a dream to dance.

•••

O Faustus talks to himself,
talks to himself, talks to himself,
talks to himself, talks to himself,
Faustus talks to himself,
talks to himself.

•••

Ikkyū's ten years near the whorehouses
shortens distances, is truly palpable;
and in ten years you will surely
get over your itch. Or not.

•••

Don't waste yourself staring at the moon.
All of those moon-staring-rear-view-mirror deaths!
Study the shadow of the horse turd in the grass.
There must be a difference between looking at a picture
of a bird and the actual bird (barn swallow)
fifteen feet from my nose on the shed eaves.
That cloud SSW looks like the underside
of a river in the sky.

•••

O I'm lucky
got a car that starts almost every day
tho' I want a new yellow Chevy pickup
got two letters today
and I'd rather have three
have a lovely wife
but want all the pretty ones
got three white hawks in the barn
but want a Himalayan eagle
have a planet in the basement
but would prefer the moon in the granary
have the northern lights
but want the Southern Cross.

      •••

The stillness of this earth
which we pass through
with the precise speed of our dreams.

      •••

I'm getting very old. If I were a mutt
in dog years I'd be seven, not stray so far.
I am large. Tarpon my age are often large
but they are inescapably fish. A porpoise
my age was the King of New Guinea in 1343.
Perhaps I am the king of my dogs, cats, horses,
but I have dropped any notion of explaining
to them why I read so much. To be mysterious
is a prerogative of kingship. I discovered
lately that my subjects do not live a life,

but are life itself. They do not recognize
the pain of the schizophrenia of kingship.
To them I am pretty much a fellow creature.

      ♦♦♦

So distances: yearns for Guayaquil and Petersburg,
the obvious Paris and Rome,
restraint in the Cotswolds, perfumes of Arusha,
Entebbe bristling with machine guns,
also Ecuadorian & Ethiopian airports,
border guards always whistling in boredom
and playing with machine guns;
all to count the flies on the lion's eyelids
and the lioness hobbling in deep grass
lacking one paw, to scan the marlin's caudal fin
cutting the Humboldt swell, an impossible scissors.

      ♦♦♦

There must be a cricket named Zagreus
in the granary tucked under a roof beam,
under which my three-year-old daughter
boogies madly,
her first taste of the Grateful Dead;
she is well out of her mind.

      ♦♦♦

Rain on the tin roof which covers a temple,
rain on my walking head which covers a temple,
rain covering my laugh shooting

toward the woods for no reason,
rain splattering in pasture's heat
raising cones of dust,
and off the horses' backs,
on oriole's nest in ash tree,
on my feet poking out the door,
testing the endurance of our actual pains,
biting hard against the sore tooth.

♦♦♦

She's rolling in the bear fat
She's rolling in the sand
She's climbing a vine
She's boarding a jet
She flies into the distance wearing blue shoes

♦♦♦

Having become the person I most feared in Childhood –
A DRUNKARD. They were pointed out to us
in our small town: oil workers, some poor farmers
(on Saturday marketing), a mechanic, a fired teacher.
They'd stumble when walking, sometimes yell
on the street at noon, wreck their old cars;
their wives would request special prayers in church,
and the children often came to school in winter
with no socks. We took up a collection to buy
the dump-picker's daughter shoes. Also my uncles
are prone to booze, also my father though it was well-
controlled, and now my fifteen-year war with the bottle
with whiskey removing me from the present

in a sweet, laughing haze, removing anger, anxiety,
instilling soft grandness, decorating ugliness
and reaffirming my questionable worth. SEE: Olson's
fingers touch his thumb, encircling the bottle – he
gulps deeply, talking through one night into the next
afternoon, talking, basking in Gorton's fishy odor.
So many of my brethren seem to die of busted guts.
Now there is a measured truce with maps and lines
drawn elegantly against the binge, concessions,
measurings, hesitant steps. My favorite two bars
are just north and barely south of the 45th parallel.

    •••

I no longer believe in the idea of magic,
christs, the self, metal buddhas, bibles.
A horse is only the space his horseness requires.
If I pissed in the woods would a tree see my ear
fall off and would the ear return to the body
on the morning of the third day? Do bo trees
ever remember the buddhas who've slept beneath them?
I admit that yesterday I built an exploratory altar.
Who can squash his delight in incomprehension?
So on a piece of old newspaper I put an earthworm
on a maple leaf, the remains of a bluebird after
the cat was finished – head and feet, some dog hair,
shavings from when we trimmed the horses' hooves,
a snakeskin, a stalk of ragweed, a gourd,
a lemon, a cedar splinter, a nonsymbolic doorknob,
a bumblebee with his juice sucked out by a wasp.
Before this altar I invented a doggerel mantra
it is this   it is this   it is this

•••

It is very hard to give birds advice.
They are already members of eternity.
In their genes they have both compass
and calendar. Their wing bones are hollow.
We are surprised by how light a dead bird is.

•••

But what am I penetrating?
Only that it seems nothing convinces
itself or anyone else reliably
of its presence. It is in the distance.

•••

No Persephone in my life,
Ariadne, Helen, Pocahontas,
Evangeline of the Book House
but others not less extraordinary who step
lightly into the dream life, refusing to leave:
girl in a green dress,
woman lolling in foot-deep Caribbean,
woman on balcony near Vatican,
girl floating across Copley Square in 1958,
mythologized woman in hut in 1951,
girl weeping in lilacs,
woman slapping my face,
girl smoking joint in bathtub looking at big toe,
slender woman eating three lobsters,
woman who blew out her heart with cocaine,

girl livid and deformed in dreams,
girl breaking the window in rage,
woman sick in hotel room,
heartless woman in photo –
not heartless but a photo.

♦♦♦

My left eye is nearly blind.
No words have ever been read with it.
Not that the eye is virgin – thirty years ago
it was punctured by glass. In everything
it sees a pastel mist. The poster of Chief Joseph
could be King Kong, Hong Kong, a naked lady riding
a donkey into Salinas, Kansas. A war atrocity.
This eye is the perfect art critic. This eye
is a perfect lover saying bodies don't matter,
it is the voice. This eye can make a lightbulb
into the moon when it chooses. Once a year I open
it to the full moon out in the pasture and yell,
white light white light.

♦♦♦

A half-dozen times a day
I climb through the electric fence
on my way and back to my study
in the barnyard. I have to be cautious.
I have learned my true dimensions,
how far my body sticks out from my brain.

♦♦♦

We are each
the only world
we are going to get.

◆◆◆

I don't want to die. It would certainly
inconvenience my wife and daughters.
I am sufficiently young that it would help
my publisher unpack his warehouse of books.
It would help me stop drinking and lose weight.
I could talk to Boris Pasternak.
He never saw the film.

◆◆◆

Wanting to pull the particular nail
that will collapse the entire house
so that there is nothing there,
not even a foundation: a rubble heap,
no sign at all, just grass, weeds and trees
among which you cannot find a shard of masonry,
which like an arrowhead might suggest
an entire civilization.

◆◆◆

She was lying back in the rowboat.
It was hot.
She tickled me with her toes.
She picked lily pads.
She watched mating dragonflies.

"How many fish below us?"
"O a hundred or so."
"It would be fun to fall in love with someone."
The rower continued his rowing.

       •••

Why be afraid of a process you're
already able to describe with precision?
To say you don't believe in it
is to say that you're *not.*
It doesn't care so why should you?
You've been given your body back
without a quarrel. See this vision
of your imagined body float toward you:
it disappears into you without a trace.
You feel full with a fullness again.
Your dimensions aren't scattered in dreams.

       •••

This fat pet bird I've kept so many years,
a crow with a malformed wing
tucked against its side, no doubt a vestigial fin:
I taught him early to drink from my whiskey
or wineglass in the shed but he prefers wine.
He flies only in circles of course
but when he drinks he flies in great
circles miles wide, preferring bad days
with low cold clouds looking like leper brains.
I barely hear his whimps & howls: O jesus
the pain O shit it hurts O god let it end.

He drags himself through air mostly landing
near a screen door slamming, a baby's cry,
a dog's bark, a forest fire, a sleeping coyote.
These fabulous memories of earth!

◆◆◆

Not to live in fancy
these short hours: let shadows
fall from walls as shadows, nothing else.
New York is exactly
dead center
in New York.
Not to indulge this heartsickness as failure.
Did I write three songs or seven
or half-a-one, one line, phrases?
A single word
that might hang in the still, black air
for more than a few moments?
Then the laughter comes again.
We *sing it away*.
What short wicks
we fuel with our blood.

◆◆◆

Disease!
My prostate beating & pulsing
down there like a frightened turkey's heart.

◆◆◆

A cold day,
low ceiling.
A cloud the size
of a Greyhound bus
just hit the house.

•••

Offenses this summer against Nature:
poured iced tea on a garter snake's head
as he or she dozed on the elm stump,
pissed on a bumblebee (inattentive),
kicked a thousand wasps to death in my slippers.
Favors done this summer for Nature:
let the mice keep their nest in the green station wagon,
let Rachel the mare breathe her hot damp horse breath
against my bare knee when she wanted to,
tried without success to get the song sparrow out
of the shed where she had trapped herself fluttering
along the cranny under the assumption that the way *out*
is always the way *up*, and her wings lie to her
with each separate beat against the ceiling saying
there is no way down and out,
there is no way down and out,
the open door back into the world.

•••

Coleridge's pet spider
he says is very intellectual,
spins webs of deceit
straight out of his big
hanging ass.

•••

Mandrill, *Mandrillus sphinx,*
crest, mane, beard, yellow, purple, green,
a large fierce, gregarious baboon –
has small wit but ties himself to a typewriter
with wolfish and bloody appetite.
He is just one, thousands will follow,
something true to be found among the countless
millions of typed pages. There's a picture
of him in Tibet though no mandrills have been known
to live there. He wants to be with his picture
though there's no way to get there. So he types.
So he dreams *lupanar lupanar lupanar*
brothels with steam and white dust, music
that describes undiscovered constellations
so precisely the astronomers of the next century
will know where to look. Peaches dripping light.
Lupanar. The female arriving in dreams is unique,
not another like her on earth; she's created for a moment.
It only happens one time. One time O one time.
He types. She's his only real food.
O *lupanar* of dreams.

•••

Head bobbing right and left,
with no effort
and for the first time
I see all sides of the pillar at once,
the earth,   her body.

259

•••

I can't jump
high anymore.

•••

He tightens
pumps in blue cold air
gasoline
the electricity from summer storms
the seven-by-seven-foot
blue face of lightning
that shot down the gravel road
like a ghost rocket.

•••

Saw the lord of crows
late at night in my living room;
don't know what true color of man –
black–white–red–yellow –
as he was hooded with the mask of a crow;
arms, legs, with primary feathers sewn to leather
downy black breast
silver bells at wrist
long feathered tail
dancing for a moment or two then disappearing.
Only in the morning did it occur to me
that it was a woman.

•••

What sways us is not each other
but our dumb insistent pulse beating
I was I am I will I was
sometimes operatic, then in church
or barroom tenor, drunkenly, in prayer,
slowly in the confusion of dreams
but the same tripartite, the three
of being here trailing off into itself,
no finale any more than a beginning
until all of us lie buried
in the stupefying ache of caskets.

♦♦♦

This earth of intentions.
Moonfucked, you can't eat or drink
or sleep at ten feet. Kneeling, love
is at nose tip. Or wound about
each other our eyes forget that they are eyes
and begin to see. You remember individual
fence posts, fish, trees, ankles,
from your tenth year.
Those savages lacking other immediate alternatives
screwed the ground to exhaustion.

♦♦♦

Bad art: walking away untouched, unmoving,
barely tickled, *amused,* diverted killing time,
throwing salt on the grass. The grace of Yukio Mishima's
suicide intervening in the false harmony,
Kawabata decides to live longer, also a harmony.

In bad music, the cheapest and easiest way to get
out of it infers Clapton. Eros girdled in metal
and ozone. A man in a vacuum of images, stirring
his skull with his dick, sparing himself his future,
fancy bound, unparticular, unpeculiar, following
the strings of his dreaming to more dreaming
in a sump narcosis, never having given himself
over to his life, never owning an instant.

    ◆◆◆

Week's eating log:
whitefish poached with lemon, onion, wine, garlic;
Chulapa – pork roasted twelve hours with pinto beans,
red peppers, chili powder; grilled twenty-two pounds
of beef ribs for friends; a lamb leg pasted with Dijon
mustard, soy, garlic; Chinese pork ribs; *menudo*
just for Benny & me as no one else would eat it –
had to cook tripe five hours then mix with hominy
and peppers with *chorizo* tacos on the side;
copious fresh vegetables, Burgundy, Columbard, booze
with all of the above; at night fevered dreams
of her sumptuous butt, a Mercator projection,
the map of an enormous meal in my brain.
Still trying to lose weight.

    ◆◆◆

How strange to see a horse
stare
straight up.

•••

Everything is a good idea at the time.
Staring with stupid longing at a picture, dumbstruck
as they used to call it, an instant's whimsy;
a body needlessly unlike any other's,
deserved by someone so monstrous
as Lucrezia Borgia: how do you come to terms
with it? thinks the American. You don't, *terms*
being a financial word not applicable
to bodies. Wisdom shies away, the packhorse
startled at the diamondback beneath the mesquite,
the beauty of threat. Now look at her as surely
as that other beast, the dead crow beneath the apple
tree so beautiful in its black glossiness
but without eyes, feet stiff and cool as the air.
I watched it for a year and owned its bleached
shinbone but gave it to someone who needed
the shinbone of a crow.

•••

She says it's too hot,
the night's too short,
that I'm too drunk,
but it's not *too* anything, ever.

•••

Living all my life with a totally normal-sized dick
(cf. the authorities: Van de Velde, Masters & Johnson)
neither hedgehog or horse, neither emu or elephant

(saw one in Kenya, the girls said O my goodness)
neither wharf rat, arrogant buck dinosaur,
prepotent swan, ground squirrel, Lauxmont Admiral
famous Holstein bull who sired 200,000 artificially.
I am saved from trying to punish anyone,
from confusing it with a gun, harpoon, cannon, sword,
cudgel, Louisville Slugger. It just sits there
in the dark, shy and friendly
like the new kid at school.

   ⋅⋅⋅

In our poetry we want to rub our nose hard
into whatever is before it; to purge
these dreams of pictures, photos, phantom people.
She offers a flex of butt, belly button, breasts,
slight puff of veneris, gap in teeth often capped,
grace of knees, high cheekbones and neck,
all the thickness of paper. The grandest illusion
as in ten thousand movies in all those hours
of dark, the only true sound the exploding
popcorn and the dairy fetor of butter. After the movie
a stack of magazines at the drugstore
to filter through, to be filtered through.

   ⋅⋅⋅

A choral piece for a dead dog:
how real the orchestra and hundred
voices on my lawn; pagan with the dog
on a high cedar platform to give the fire
its full marriage of air; the chorus

sings DOG a thousand times, dancing
in a circle. That would be a proper
dog funeral. By god. No dreams here
but a mighty shouting of *dog*.

♦♦♦

Sunday night,
I'm lucky to have all of this vodka,
a gift of Stolichnaya.
And books. And a radio
playing WSM all the way from Nashville.
Four new pups in the bedroom.
The house snores. My tooth aches.
It is time to fry an egg.

♦♦♦

Heard the foghorn out at sea,
saw horses' backs shiny with rain,
felt my belly jiggle as I walked
through the barnyard in a light rain
with my daughter's small red umbrella
to protect the not-very-precious manuscript,
tiptoeing barefoot in the tall wet grass
trying to avoid the snakes.

♦♦♦

With all this rain
the pond is full.
The ducks are one week old

and already speak their language perfectly —
a soft nasal hiss.
With no instructions they skim bugs from the pond's
surface and look fearfully at me.

♦♦♦

The minister whacks off as does the insurance man,
habitual golfer, sweet lady in her bower,
as do novelists, monks, nuns in nunneries,
maidens in dormitories, stallion against fence post,
goat against puzzled pig who does not cease feeding,
and so do senators, generals, wives during TV
game shows, movie stars and football players, students
to utter distraction, teachers, butchers, world leaders,
everyone except poets who fear the dreaded
growth of hair on the palms, blindness.
They know that even in an empty hotel room
in South Dakota that someone is watching.

♦♦♦

With my dog
I watched a single crow
fly across the field.
We are each one.

♦♦♦

Thirty feet up in the air
near the top of my novel I want a bird to sing
from the crown of the barn roof.

A hundred feet away there is a grove of trees,
maple and elm and ash,
placed quite accidentally before any of us were born.
Everyone remembers who planted the lilacs
forty years and three wars ago.

♦♦♦

In the morning paper
the arsonist
who was also a paranoid schizophrenic,
a homosexual,
retarded,
an alcoholic
who lacerated his body with a penknife
and most significantly for the rest of us,
started fires where none where desired,
on whim.

♦♦♦

Spent months regathering dreams lost in the diaspora,
all of the prism's colors, birds, animals, bodies,
getting them back within the skin
where they'd do no damage.
How difficult catching them armed
only with a butterfly-catcher's net,
a gun, airplane, an ice pick,
a chalice of rainwater, a green headless
buddha on loan from a veteran of foreign wars.

♦♦♦

Saw that third eye in a dream
but couldn't remember if it looked
from a hole in a wall of ice,
or a hole in a floor of ice,
but it was an eye looking from a hole in ice.

•••

Two white-faced cattle out in the dark-green pasture,
one in the shade of the woodlot,
one out in the hot sunlight,
eating slowly and staring at each other.

•••

So exhausted after my walk from orchestrating
the moves of one billion August grasshoppers
plus fifty thousand butterflies
swimming at the heads
of fifty thousand wildflowers
red blue yellow orange
orange flowers the only things that rhyme with orange
the one rabbit in the pasture
one fly buzzing at the window
a single hot wind through the window
a man sitting at my desk resembling me.

•••

He sneaks up on the temple slowly at noon.
He's so slow it seems like it's taking years.
Now his hands are on a pillar, the fingers
encircling it, with only the tips inside the gate.

•••

After all of this long moist dreaming
I perceive how accurate the rooster's crow
is from down the road.

•••

You can suffer and not even know you're suffering
because you've been suffering so long you can't remember
another life. You're actually a dead dog on a country road.
And a man gets used to his rotten foot.
After a while it's simply a rotten foot,
and his rotten ideas are even easier to get used to
because they don't hurt as much as a rotten foot.
The road from Belsen to Watergate paved
with perfectly comfortable ideas, ideas to sleep on
like a mattress stuffed with money and death,
an actual waterbed filled with liquid gold.
So our inept tuna cravings and Japan's (she imitates
our foulest features) cost an annual
250,000 particular dolphin deaths,
certainly as dear as people to themselves
or so the evidence says.

•••

Near my lover's old frame house with a field
behind it, the grass is a brilliant gold.
Standing on the gravel road before the house
a great flock of blackbirds coming over so close

to my head I see them all individually,
eyes, crests, the feet drawn out in flight.

•••

I owe the dentist nine hundred dollars.
This is more than I made on three
of my books of poems. But then I am gloriously
free. I can let my mouth rot and quit
writing poems. I could let the dentist
write the poems while I walked into the dark
with a tray of golden teeth I'd sculpt
for myself in the forms of shark's teeth,
lion's teeth, teeth of grizzly and python.
Watch me open my mouth as I wear these wondrous
teeth. The audience gross is exactly nine hundred!
The house lights dim. My lips part.
There is a glimpse of sun.

•••

Abel always votes.
Cain usually thinks better of it
knowing not very deep in his heart
that no one deserves to be encouraged.
Abel has a good job & is a responsible screw,
but many intelligent women seem drawn
to Crazy Horse, a descendant of Cain,
even if he only gets off his buffalo pony
once a year to throw stones at the moon.
Of course these women marry Abel but at bars and parties

they are the first to turn to the opening door
to see who is coming in.

♦♦♦

I was standing near the mow door
in the darkness, a party going on in the château.
She was there with her sister.
We kissed then lay down on fresh straw in a paddock.
An angry stallion jumped over on top of us.
I could see his outline clearly against the sky.
Why did we die so long ago.

♦♦♦

How wind, cloud and water
blaspheme symmetry at every instant,
forms that can't be remembered and stored:
Grand Marais, Cape Ann at Eastern Point,
Lake Manyara from a cliff, Boca Grande's sharks
giving still water a moving shape – they are there
and there and there – the waterfall next to a girl
so obviously on a white horse, to mud
puddle cat avoids, back to Halibut Point,
Manitou convulsed in storms to thousand-mile
weed line in Sargasso Sea to brown violent confluence
of Orinoco and ocean off Devil's Gate; mixing wind,
cloud, water, the purest mathematics of their
description studied as glyphs, alchemists
everywhere working with humble gold, somewhere to begin,
having to keep eyes closed to wind, cloud, water.

•••

Saw an ox. A black horse I recognized.
A procession of carts full of flowers
pulled by nothing. Asymmetrical planets.
Fish out of their element of water.
Simple music – a single note an hour.
How are we to hear it, if at all?
No music in statement, the lowest denominator
by which our fragments can't find each other.
But I can still hear the notes of April,
the strained, fragile notes of March:
convalescent, tentative, a weak drink
taken over and over in immense doses.
It is the body that is the suite entire,
brain firmly fused to the trunk, spine
more actual than mountains, brain moving
as a river, governed precisely by her energies.

•••

Whippoorwill. Mourning dove. Hot morning rain
changing to a violent squall coming SSW out of the lake,
thunder enveloping itself then unfolding
as cloth in wind furls, holds back, furls again;
running nearly naked in shorts to my shed,
thunder rattling windows and walls,
acorns rattling against barn's tin roof;
the floor shudders, then stillness as squall passes,
as strange as a strong wind at summer twilight
when the air is yellow. Now cool still air.

Mourning dove.
Oriole.

♦♦♦

O my darling sister
O she crossed over
she's crossed over
is planted now near her father
six feet under earth's skin –
their still point on this whirling earth
now and I think forever.

♦♦♦

Now it is as close to you as the clothes you wear.
The clothes are attached to your body
by a cord that runs up your spine, out your neck
and through the earth, back up your spine.

♦♦♦

At nineteen I began to degenerate,
slight smell of death in my gestures,
unbelieving, tentative, wailing...
so nineteen years have gone. It doesn't matter.
It might have taken fifty. Or never.
Now the barriers are dissolving, the stone fences
in shambles. I want to have my life
in cloud shapes, water shapes, wind shapes,
crow call, marsh hawk swooping over grass and weed tips.
Let the scavenger take what he finds.
Let the predator love his prey.

NEW POEMS
FROM SELECTED
& NEW POEMS

to John and Rebecca

1982

NOT WRITING MY NAME

In the snow, that is. The "J" could have been
three hundred yards into the high pasture
across the road. The same with the "I" which I intended
to dot by sprawling and flopping in a drift. The "M"
naturally would have required something more
than twelve hundred yards of hard walking as we
have two empty-bottomed isosceleses to deal with.
What star-crossed jock ego would churn through those
drifts to write a name invisible except to crows?
And the dog would have confused the crows the way
he first runs ahead, then crisscrosses my path.
It's too cold anyhow – ten below at noon though the sun
would tell me otherwise. And the wind whips coils
and wisps of snow across the hardened drifts and around
my feet like huge ghost snakes. These other signatures:
Vole tracks so light I have to kneel to trace his
circlings which are his name. Vole. And an unknown bird,
scarcely heavier than the vole, that lacks a left foot. Fox tracks
leading up a drift onto my favorite boulder where he swished
his tail, definitely peed, and left. The dog sniffs
the tracks, also pees but sparingly. He might need it later,
he saves his messages. For a moment mastodons float
through the trees, thunderhead colored, stuffing their maws
with branches. This place used to be Africa. Now it's so cold
there are blue shadows in my footprints, and a blue-shadow
dog runs next to my own, flat and rippling to the snow, less than
paper thick. I try to invoke a crow for company; none appears.
I have become the place the crow didn't appear.

FROG

First memory
of swimming underwater:
eggs of frogs hanging in diaphanous clumps
from green lily pad stems;
at night in the tent I heard
the father of it all booming
and croaking in the reeds.

ROOSTER

to Pat Ryan

I have to kill the rooster tomorrow. He's being an asshole,
having seriously wounded one of our two hens with his insistent banging.
You walk into the barn to feed the horses and pick up an egg
or two for breakfast and he jumps her proclaiming *she's mine she's mine.*
Her wing is torn and the primary feathers won't grow back.
Chickens have largely been denatured, you know. He has no part
in those delicious fresh eggs. He crows on in a vacuum. He is
utterly pointless. He's as dumb as a tapeworm and no one cares
if he lives or dies. There. I can kill him
with an easy mind. But I'm still not up to it. Maybe I can hire
a weasel or a barn rat to do the job, or throw him to Justine,
the dog, who would be glad to rend him except the neighbors
have chickens too, she'd get the habit and we would have a beloved shot
dog to bury. So he deserves to die, having no purpose. We'll
have stewed barnyard chicken, closer to eating a gamebird than
that tasteless supermarket chicken born and bred in a caged
darkness. Everything we eat is dead except an occasional oyster
or clam. Should I hire the neighbor boy to kill him? Will the
hens stop laying out of grief? Isn't his long wavering crow
magnificent? Isn't the worthless rooster the poet's bird brother?
No. He's just a rooster and the world has no place for him.
Should I wait for a full wintry moon, take him to the top of the
hill after dropping three hits of mescaline and strangle him?
Should I set him free for a fox meal? They're coming back now
after the mange nearly wiped them out. He's like a leaking roof
with drops falling on my chest. He's the Chinese torture in the barn.
He's lust mad. His crow penetrates walls. His head bobs in lunar
jerks. The hens shudder but are bored with the pain of eggs.

What can I do with him? Nothing isn't enough. In the morning we will sit down together and talk it out. I will tell him he doesn't matter and he will wag his head, strut, perhaps crow.

EPITHALAMIUM

for Peter and Maria

For the first time the wind
blew straight down from the heavens.
I was wandering around the barnyard
about three AM in full moonlight
when it started, flattening my hair
against my head; my dog cowered
between my knees, and the last leaves
of a cold November shot to the ground.
Then the wind slowed and went back to the north.
This happened last night and already at noon
my faith in it is passing.

A REDOLENCE FOR NIMS

O triple sob – turned forty
at midnight – body at dawn
booze-soddened but hopeful,
knowing that the only thing
to remember is dreams.
Dead clear zero, Sunday afternoon
in an attic of a closed resort
on Lake Michigan with one lone
duck riding the diminishing
swells of yesterday's storm
against the snowy cliffs of North Manitou:
Whom are we to love?
How many and what for?
My heart's gone to sea for years.
This is a prayer, plaint, wish,
howl of void beneath breastbone.
Dreams, soul chasers, bring
back my heart alive.

FOLLOWERS

Driving east on buddha's birthday,
April 9, 1978, past my own birthplace
Grayling, Michigan, south 300 miles to Toledo,
then east again to New York for no reason –
belled heart swinging in grief for months
until I wanted to take my life in my hands;
three crows from home followed above
the car until the Delaware River where
they turned back: one stood all black
and lordly on a fresh pheasant killed
by a car: all this time
counting the mind, counting crows,
each day's ingredients
the same, barring rare
bad luck
good luck
dumb luck
all set in marble by the habitual,
locked as the day passes moment by moment:
say on the tracks the train can't
turn 90 degrees to the right because it's not
the nature of a train,
but we think a man can dive
in a pond, swim across it,
and climb a tree though few of us do.

MY FIRST DAY AS A PAINTER

Things to paint:
my dog (yellow),
nude women,
dead coyote with gray whiskers,
nude women,
a tree full of crows,
nude women,
the self in the mirror,
nude women,
a favorite cloud,
nude women,
a worn-out scalpel,
nude women,
dead friends,
nude women ages 14–80 (12–82),
call me wherever you are at noon
in the glory of noon light,
bring your dogs and birds,
everybody is welcome:
nude women spinning in godlike whirls
creating each other in endless
streams of human eggs!

WAITING

There are no calls from the outside.
Miracles are the perversity of literature.
We should know that by now.
Only that these never-revealed connections of things
lead us oddly on. Caesar's legions
entering Greenland's ice, the scout far in front
wanting to do battle where there are
no enemies,
never were any enemies.

NOON

Spring: despondency,
fall: despair,
onset of winter
a light rain in the heart
the pony tethered to the telephone
pole day after day until he's eaten
the circle, moved to another pole,
another circle: winter never deepens
but falls dead upon the ground,
body of the sky whirled
in gray gusts:
from Manitoba stretched brains
of north; heat for heart, head,
in smallest things – dry socks,
strange breasts, an ounce of sun
glittering above the blue shadows
of the barn.

BIRTHDAY

The masques of dream – monk in his
lineage – what does he wear to shield
himself? First shield made of a cloud,
second – a tree, third – a shadow; and
leading to the stretched coils of light
(how they want to gather us up
with our permission), three men.
Two dead tho' dead is supernumerary.
The cause is the effect.
He laughed like a lake would
but only once, never twice into the same
mystery. Not ever to stop but only
to drop the baggage, to shed the
thirty-ninth skin.

CLEAR WATER 3

Ah, yes. Fame never got anyone
off the hook, it seems. Some poignant
evidence to be offered here in McGuane.
There's a cutoff beyond which a certain
number of people know you exist for various
reasons, good or bad or with a notorious
indifference.   Said Spicer:
My vocabulary did this to me. Meaning
what he was, near death in an alcoholic ward.
Crane or Cavafy. Alcohol as biography
more surely than serial poems. I doubt it.
We are drawn to where we end like water
for reasons of character, volume, gravity,
the sound we make in passing/not all the sounds
we made in passing in one place – a book.
Each day's momentum of voice carrying
backward and forward to the limits, beginning
and end. We drink to enchant our voices,
to heal them, to soothe with laughter, to glide
awhile. My words kill, killed, me, my lord. Yes.

DŌGEN'S DREAM

What happens when the god of spring
meets spring? He thinks for a moment
of great whales traveling from the bottom
to the top of the earth, the day the voyage
began seven million years ago
when spring last changed its season.
He enters himself, emptiness
desiring emptiness. He sleeps
and his sleep is the dance of all the birds
on earth flying north.

WEEPING

for Dave Kelly from long ago

Six days of clouds since
I returned from Montana,
a state of mind out West.
A bleak afternoon in the granary killing flies and wasps.
Sitting on a *zafu* watching flies.
Two days ago a sandhill crane flew over
so low I could see an eyeball clearly cocked
toward my singular own.
As I drink I miss more flies.
I am searching out the ecstatic life
with flyswatter and wineglass in hand,
the sky above an inverted steel sink.
I am looking for weeping
which is a superior form of rest.
Can't there be dry weeping? Nope.
Dry weeping is like dry fucking
which most of us remember as unsatisfying.
Wet fucking is another story
but not the object here, though decidedly
more interesting than weeping.
I would frankly like to throw
myself around and have some real passion.
Some wet passion! to be sure.
At nineteen in 1957 on Grove Street in NY
I could weep about art, Hart Crane, my empty
stomach, homesickness for pheasants and goldenrod,
Yesenin's suicide, a red-haired girl with an improbable
butt, my dad planting the garden alone.
It was a year in which I wrung out pillowcases at dawn.

But this is the flip side of the record, a log
of the search for weeping. I've been dry
for a decade and it isn't panning out.
Like a Hollywood producer I sit by a pool
and hatch inane plots against the weeping imagination,
spinning wheels, treading water,
beating the mental bishop,
flogging the mental clam,
pulling the mental wire
like a cub scout in a lonely pup tent.
I'm told I laugh too much.
I laugh deeply at Johnny Carson monologues,
at my poetry, at health food & politics,
at the tragic poetry of others, at the weedy garden,
at my dog hitting the electric fence,
at women freeing themselves when I am in bondage,
at the thought of my death.
In fact I'm tickled pink with life.
I actually have a trick to weep but it's cheating.
I used it once when I was very drunk.
I thought of the deaths of my wife and daughters.
I threw myself to the floor weeping.
I wept horribly and shook, gnashed my teeth.
I must die before them.

THE CHATHAM GHAZAL

It is the lamp on the kitchen table
well after midnight saying nothing but light.

Here are a list of ten million measurements.
You may keep them. Or throw them away.

A strange warm day when November has forgotten
to be November. Birds form shrill clouds.

Phototropiques. We emerge upward from liquid.
See the invisible husks we've left behind called memories.

The press wonders how we drink so much poison and stay
alive. The antidote is chance, mobility, sleeplessness.

They've killed another cow. With the mountain of guts
I also bury all of the skins of thirty-seven years.

MARRIAGE GHAZAL

for Peter & Beck

Hammering & drifting. Sea wrack. Cast upon & cast out.
Who's here but shore? Where we stop is where shore is.

I saw the light beyond mountains turned umber by morning.
I walked by memory as if I had no legs. Or head.

In a bed of reeds I found my body and entered it,
taking my life upon myself, the soul made comfortable.

So the body's a nest for the soul and we set out inland,
the figure of a walker who only recognized the sea and moon.

And coming to the first town the body became a chorus –
O my god this is a place or thing and I'll stay awhile.

The body met a human with fur and the moon mounted her head
in an arc when she sat & they built a boat together.

MARCH WALK

I was walking because I wasn't upstairs sitting.
I could have been looking for pre-1900 gold coins
in the woods all afternoon. What a way to make a living!
The same mastodon was there only three hundred years from
where I last saw him. I felt the sabers on the saber tooth,
the hot wet breath on the back of my hand. Three deer
and a number of crows, how many will remain undisclosed:
It wasn't six and it wasn't thirty. There were four girls
ranging back to 1957. The one before that just arrived
upstairs. There was that long morose trip into the world
hanging onto my skin for a quarter of a mile, shed with some
difficulty. There was one dog, my own, and one grouse
not my own. A strong wind flowed over and through us like
dry water. I kissed a scar on a hip. I found a rotting
crab apple and a distant relative to quartz. You could spend
a lifetime and still not walk to an island. I met none of the
dead today having released them yesterday at three o'clock.
If you're going to make love to a woman you have to give
her some of your heart. Else don't. If I had found a gold coin
I might have left it there with my intermittent interest in
money. The dead snipe wasn't in the same place but the rocks
were. The apple tree was a good place to stand. Every late fall
the deer come there for dessert. They will stand for days
waiting for a single apple to tumble from the upmost limb.

THE WOMAN FROM SPIRITWOOD

Sleeping from Mandan to Jamestown,
waking near Spiritwood in the van,
shrinking in fever with the van
buffeted by wind so that it shudders,
the wind maybe fifty knots straight N by NW
out of Saskatchewan. Stopping for gas we see men
at the picnic tables cleaning the geese they've shot:
October first with the feathers carried off by the wind
into fields where buffalo once roamed, also
the Ogalala & Miniconjou Sioux roamed in search
of buffalo and Crazy Horse on a horse that outlived him.
She comes out of the station, smiling, leaning into the wind.
She is so beautiful than an invisible hand reaches
into your rib cage and twists your heart one notch
counterclockwise. There is nowhere to go.
I've been everywhere and there's nowhere to go.
The talk is halting, slow until it becomes
the end of another part of the future.
I scratch gravel toward and from this wound,
seeing within the shadow that this shadow casts
how freedom must be there
before there can be freedom.

GATHERING APRIL

for Simic

Stuffing a crow call in one ear
and an unknown bird's in the other,
lying on the warm cellar door out of
the cool wind which I take small sparing
bites of with three toes still wet from the pond's
edge: April is so violent up here you hide
in corners or, when in the woods, in swales
and behind beech trees. Twenty years ago
this April I offered my stupid heart up to
this bloody voyage. It was near a marsh
on a long walk. You can't get rid of those
thousand pointless bottles of whiskey
that you brought along. Last night after
the poker game I read Obata's Li Po.
He was no less a fool but adding those
twenty thousand poems you come up
with a god. There are patents on all
the forms of cancer but still we praise
god from whom or which all blessings flow:
that an April exists, that a body lays itself
down on a warm cellar door and remembers, drinks
in birds and wind, whiskey, frog songs
from the marsh, the little dooms hiding
in the shadow of each fence post.

WALTER OF BATTERSEA

for Anjelica

I shall commit suicide or die
trying, Walter thought beside
the Thames – at low tide and very
feminine.

Picture him: a cold November day,
the world through a long lens; he's
in new blue pants and races the river
for thirty-three steps.

Walter won. Hands down. Then lost
again. Better to die trying! The sky
so bleak. God blows his nose above
the Chelsea Flour Mills.

What is he at forty, Nov. 9, 1978, so far
from home: grist for his own mill; all
things have become black–and–white
without hormonal surge.

And religious. He's forgiven god
for the one hundred ladies who turned him
down and took him up. O that song –
I asked her for water and she gave
me kerosene.

No visions of Albion, no visions at all,
in fact, the still point of the present winding

about itself, graceful, unsnarled. I am
here today and gone tomorrow.

How much is he here? Not quite with
all his heart and soul. Step lightly
or the earth revolves into a berserk
spin. Fall off or dance.

And choosing dance not god, at least
for the time being. Things aren't what
they seem but what they are – infinitely
inconsolable.

He knows it's irony that's least
valuable in this long deathwatch.
Irony scratching its tired ass. No trade-offs
with time and fortune.

It's indelicate to say things twice except
in prayer. The drunk repeats to keep
his grasp, a sort of prayer: the hysteria
of the mad, a verbless prayer.

Walter recrossed the bridge which was
only a bridge. He heard his footsteps
just barely behind him. The river is not
where it starts and ends.

AFTER READING TAKAHASHI

for Lucien, Peter, and Whalen

Nothing is the same to anyone.
Moscow is east of Nairobi
but thinks of herself as perpetually west.
The bird sees the top of my head,
an even trade for her feathered belly.
Our eyes staring through the nose bridge
never to see each other.
She is not I, I not her.
So what, you think, having little
notion of my concerns. O that dank
basement of "so what" known by all
though never quite the same way.
All of us drinking through a cold afternoon,
our eyes are on the mirror behind
the bottles, on the snow out the window
which the wind chases fruitlessly,
each in his separateness drinking,
talk noises coming out of our mouths.
In the corner a pretty girl plays pinball.
I have no language to talk to her.
I have come to the point in life when
I could be her father. This was never true before.
The bear hunter talked about the mountains.
We looked at them together out of the
tavern window in Emigrant, Montana.
He spent fifty years in the Absaroka Mountains
hunting grizzly bears and, at one time, wolves.
We will never see the same mountains.
He knows them like his hands, his wife's

breasts and legs, his old dog sitting outside
in the pickup. I only see beautiful mountains
and say "beautiful mountains" to which he nods
graciously but they are a photo of China to me.
And all lessons are fatal: the great snowy owl
that flew in front of me so that
I ducked in the car; it will never happen again.
I've been warned by a snowy night, an owl,
the infinite black above and below me to look
at all creatures and things with a billion eyes,
not struggling with the single heartbeat
that is my life.

THE THEORY &
PRACTICE OF RIVERS
& NEW POEMS

In Memoriam
GLORIA ELLEN HARRISON
1964–1979

1985, 1989

THE THEORY AND PRACTICE OF RIVERS

The rivers of my life:
moving looms of light,
anchored beneath the log
at night I can see the moon
up through the water
as shattered milk, the nudge
of fishes, belly and back
in turn grating against log
and bottom; and letting go, the current
lifts me up and out
into the dark, gathering motion,
drifting into an eddy
with a sideways swirl,
the sandbar cooler than the air:
to speak it clearly,
how the water goes
is how the earth is shaped.

It is not so much that I got
there from here, which is everyone's
story: but the shape
of the voyage, how it pushed
outward in every direction
until it stopped:
roots of plants and trees,
certain coral heads,
photos of splintered lightning,
blood vessels,
the shapes of creeks and rivers.

This is the ascent out of water:
there is no time but that
of convenience, time so that everything
won't happen at once; dark
doesn't fall – dark comes up
out of the earth, an exhalation.
It gathers itself close
to the ground, rising
to envelop us, as if the bottom
of the sea rose up to meet us.
Have you ever gone
to the bottom of the sea?

Mute unity of water.
I sculpted this girl
out of ice so beautifully
she was taken away.
How banal the swan song
which is a water song.
There never was a swan
who said good-bye. My raven
in the pine tree squawked his way
to death, falling from branch
to branch. To branch again.
To ground. The song, the muffle
of earth as the body falls,
feather against pine needles.

Near the estuary north of Guilford
my brother recites the Episcopalian
burial service over his dead daughter.

Gloria, as in *Gloria in Excelsis*.
I cannot bear this passion and courage;
my eyes turn toward the swamp
and sea, so blurred they'll never quite
clear themselves again. The inside of the eye,
vitreous humor, is the same pulp found
inside the squid. I can see Gloria
in the snow and in the water. She lives
in the snow and water and in my eyes.
This is a song for her.

Kokopele saved me this time:
flute song in soft dark
sound of water over rock,
the moon glitter rippling;
breath caught as my hunched
figure moved in a comic circle,
seven times around the cabin
through the woods in the dark.
Why did I decide to frighten myself?

Light snow in early May,
wolf prints in alluvial fan,
moving across the sandbar
in the river braided near its mouth
until the final twist; then the prints
move across drift ice in a dead
channel, and back into the swamp.

The closest I came to describing it:
it is early winter, mid-November

with light snow, the ground rock-hard
with frost. We are moving but I can't
seem to find my wife and two daughters.
I have left our old house and can't remember
how to find the new one.

The days are stacked against
what we think we are:
the story of the water babies
swimming up- and downstream
amid waterweed, twisting
with cherubic smiles in the current,
human and fish married.
Again! The girl I so painfully
sculpted out of ice
was taken away. She said:
"Goddamn the Lizard King,"
her night message and good-bye.
The days are stacked against
what we think we are:
near the raven rookery
inside the bend of river
with snowmelt and rain
flooding the bend; I've failed to stalk
these birds again and they flutter
and wheel above me with parental screams
saying, *Get out get out you bastard.*
The days are stacked against
what we think we are.
After a month of interior weeping
it occurred to me that in times like these

I have nothing to fall back on
except the sun and moon and earth.
I dress in camouflage and crawl
around swamps and forest, seeing
the bitch coyote five times but never
before she sees me. Her look
is curious, almost a smile.
The days are stacked against
what we think we are:
it is nearly impossible
to surprise ourselves.
I will never wake up
and be able to play the piano.
South fifteen miles, still
near the river, calling coyotes
with Dennis E: full moon in east,
northern lights in pale green swirl,
from the west an immense line squall
and thunderstorm approaching off Lake Superior.
Failing with his call he uses
the song of the loon to bring
an answer from the coyotes.
"They can't resist it," he says.
The days are stacked against
what we think we are.
Standing in the river up to my waist
the infant beaver peeks at me
from the flooded tag alder
and approaches though warned
by her mother whacking her tail.
About seven feet away she bobs

to dive, mooning me with her small
pink ass, rising again for another
look, then downward swimming
past my leg, still looking.
The days are finally stacked
against what we think we are:
how long can I stare at the river?
Three months in a row now
with no signs of stopping,
glancing to the right, an almost
embarrassed feeling that the river
will stop flowing and I can go home.
The days, at last, are stacked against
what we think we are.
Who in their most hallowed, sleepless
night with the moon seven feet
outside the window, the moon
that the river swallows, would wish
it otherwise?

On New Year's Eve I'm wrapped
in my habits, looking up to the TV
to see the red ball, the apple,
rise or fall, I forget which:
a poem on the cherry-wood table, a fire,
a blizzard, some whiskey, three
restless cats, and two sleeping dogs,
at home and making three gallons
of *menudo* for the revelers who'll
need it come tomorrow after amateur night:
about ten pounds of tripe, ancho,

molida, serrano, and chipotle pepper, cumin,
coriander, a few calves' or piglets' feet.
I don't wonder what is becoming
to the man already becoming.
I also added a half-quart of stock
left over from last night's *bollito misto*
wherein I poach for appropriate times:
fifteen pounds of veal bones to be discarded,
a beef brisket, a pork roast, Italian sausage,
a large barnyard hen, a pheasant, a guinea
hen, and for about thirty minutes until
rosy rare a whole filet, served with
three sauces: tomato coulis, piquante (anchovies & capers etc.)
and a rouille. Last week when my daughter
came home from NYC I made her venison
with truffles, also roast quail for Christmas
breakfast, also a wild turkey, some roast mallards & grouse,
also a cacciatore of rabbit & pheasant.
Oddly the best meal of the year
was in the cabin by the river:
a single fresh brook trout *au bleu*
with one boiled new potato and one
wild-leek vinaigrette. By the river
I try to keep alive, perhaps to write
more poems, though lately I think
of us all as lay-down comedians
who, when we finally tried to get up,
have found that our feet are mushy,
and what's more, no one cares
or bothers to read anymore those
sotto voce below-radar flights

from the empirical. But I am wrapped
in my habits. I must send my prayer
upward and downward. "Why do you write
poems?" the stewardess asked. "I guess
it's because every angel is terrible,
still though, alas, I invoke these almost
deadly birds of the soul,"
I cribbed from Rilke.

The travels on dry riverbeds: Salt River,
or nearly dry up Canyon de Chelly,
a half-foot of water – a skin over
the brown riverbed. The Navajo
family stuck with a load of dry
corn and crab apples. Only the woman
speaks English, the children at first shy
and frightened of my blind left eye
(some tribes attach importance to this –
strangely enough, this eye can see underwater).
We're up on the del Muerto fork and while
I'm kneeling in the water shoving rocks
under the axle I glance skyward
at an Anasazi cliff dwelling, the "ancient
ones" they're called. This morning
a young schizophrenic Navajo attacked
our truck with a club, his head seeming
to turn nearly all the way around as
an owl's. Finally the children smile
as the truck is pulled free. I am given
a hatful of the most delicious crab apples
in the world. I watch the first apple

core float west on the slender current,
my throat a knot of everything
I no longer understand.

Sitting on the bank, the water
stares back so deeply you can hear
it afterward when you wish. It is the water
of dreams, and for the nightwalker
who can almost walk on the water,
it is most of all the water of awakening,
passing with the speed of life
herself, drifting in circles in an eddy
joining the current again
as if the eddy were a few moments' sleep.

The story can't hesitate to stop.
I can't find a river in Los Angeles
except the cement one behind Sportsman's Lodge
on Ventura. There I feel my
high blood pressure like an electric tiara
around my head, a small comic cloud,
a miniature junkyard where my confused
desires, hopes, hates, and loves short circuit
in little puffs of hissing ozone. And the women
are hard green horses disappearing,
concealing themselves in buildings and tops
of wild palms in ambush.
A riverless city of redolent
and banal sobs, green girls
in trees, girls hard as basalt.
"My grandfather screwed me

when I was seven years old,"
she said, while I looked out
at the cement river flowing with dusty rain,
at three dogs playing in the cement river.
"He's dead now so there's no point
sweating it," she added.

Up in the Amazon River Basin
during a dark time Matthiessen built
a raft with a native, chewed some coca leaves,
boarded the raft and off they went on a river
not on any map, uncharted, wanting to see
the Great Mother of Snakes; a truncated
version of our voyage of seventy years –
actuarial average. To see green and live green,
moving on water sometimes clouded often clear.
Now our own pond is white with ice.
In the barnyard lying in the snow
I can hear the underground creek,
a creek without a name.

I forgot to tell you that while
I was away my heart broke
and I became not so much old, but older,
definably older within a few days.
This happened on a cold dawn in New Iberia
while I was feeding a frightened stray
dog a sack of pork rinds in the rain.

Three girls danced the "Cotton-Eyed Joe,"
almost sedate, erect, with relentless grace,

where did they come from
and where did they go
in ever-so-delicate circles?
And because of time, circles
that no longer close
or return to themselves.

I rode the gray horse
all day in the rain.
The fields became unmoving rivers,
the trees foreshortened.
I saw a girl in a white dress
standing half-hidden in the water
behind a maple tree.
I pretended not to notice
and made a long slow circle
behind a floating hedgetop
to catch her unawares.
She was gone but I had that prickly
fear someone was watching from a tree,
far up in a leaf-veil of green maple leaves.
Now the horse began swimming
toward higher ground, from where
I watched the tree until dark.

"Life, this vastly mysterious process
to which our culture inures us
lest we become useless citizens!
And is it terrible to be lonely and ill?"
she wrote. "Not at all, in fact, it is better
to be lonely when ill. To others, friends,

relatives, loved ones, death is our most
interesting, our most dramatic act.
Perhaps the best thing I've learned
from these apparently cursed and bedraggled
Indians I've studied all these years
is how to die. Last year I sat beside
a seven-year-old Hopi girl as she sang
her death song in a slight quavering
voice. Who among us whites, child
or adult, will sing while we die?"

On White Fish Bay, the motor broke down
in heavy seas. We chopped ice off the gunwales
quite happily as it was unlikely we'd survive
and it was something to do. Ted just sat there
out of the wind and spray, drinking whiskey.
"I been on the wagon for a year. If I'm going
to die by god at least I get to have a drink."

What is it to actually go outside the nest
we have built for ourselves, and earlier
our father's nest: to go into a forest
alone with our eyes open? It's different
when you don't know what's over the hill –
keep the river on your left, then you see
the river on your right. I have simply
forgotten left and right, even up and down,
whirl then sleep on a cloudy day to forget
direction. It is hard to learn how
to be lost after so much training.

In New York I clocked
seven tugboats on the East River
in less than a half hour;
then I went to a party
where very rich people
talked about their arches,
foot arches, not architectural arches.
Back at my post I dozed
and saw only one more tugboat
before I slept.

But in New York I also saw a big hole
of maddened pipes with all the direction
of the swastika and a few immigrants
figuring it all out with the impenetrable
good sense of those who do the actual
work of the world.

How did I forget that rich turbulent
river, so cold in the rumply brown folds
of spring; by August cool, clear, glittery
in the sunlight; umbrous as it dips
under the logjam. In May, the river
a roar beyond a thin wall of sleep, with
the world of snow still gliding in rivulets
down imperceptible slopes; in August
through the screened window against which
bugs and moths scratch so lightly,
as lightly as the river sounds.

How can I renew oaths
I can't quite remember?
In New Orleans I was light in body and soul
because of food poisoning, the bathroom gymnastics
of flesh against marble floor,
seeing the underside of the bathtub
for the first time since I was a child,
and the next day crossing Cajun bridges
in the Atchafalaya, where blacks were thrown
to alligators I'm told, black souls whirling
in brown water, whirling
in an immaculate crawfish
rosary.

In the water I can remember
women I didn't know: Adriana
dancing her way home at the end
of a rope, a cool Tuscany night,
the apple tree in bloom;
the moon which I checked
was not quite full, a half-moon,
the rest of the life abandoned to the dark.

I warned myself all night
but then halfway between my ears
I turned toward the heavens
and reached the top of my head.
From there I can go just about
anywhere I want and I've never
found my way back home.

This isn't the old song
of the suicidal house,
I forgot the tune about small
windows growing smaller, the door
neither big enough to enter
or exit, the sinking hydraulic ceilings
and the attic full of wet cement.
I wanted to go to the Camargue,
to Corsica, to return to Costa Rica,
but I couldn't escape the suicidal house
until May when I drove
through the snow to reach the river.

On the bank by the spring creek
my shadow seemed to leap
up to gather me, or it leapt
up to gather me, not seeming so
but as a natural fact. Faulkner said
that the drowned man's shadow had watched
him from the river all the time.

Drowning in the bourgeois trough,
a *bourride* or gruel of money, drugs,
whiskey, hotels, the dream coasts,
ass in the air at the trough, drowning
in a river of pus, pus of civilization,
pus of cities, unholy river of shit,
of filth, shit of nightmares, shit
of skewed dreams and swallowed years.
The river pulls me out,
draws me elsewhere

and down to blue water,
green water,
black water.

How far between the Virgin
and the Garrison and back?
Why is it a hundred times farther to get back,
the return upriver in the dark?
It isn't innocence, but to win back breath,
body heat, the light that gathers around
a waking animal. Ten years ago I saw
the dancing Virgin in a basement
in New York, a whirl of hot color
from floor to ceiling, whirling in a dance.
At eighteen in New York
on Grove Street I discovered
red wine, garlic, Rimbaud,
and a red-haired girl. Livid colors
not known in farm country,
also Charlie Parker, Sonny Rollins,
the odors from restaurant vents,
thirty-five-cent Italian sausages
on Macdougal, and the Hudson River:
days of river-watching and trying
to get on a boat for the tropics and see
that Great Ocean river, the Gulf Stream.
Another fifteen years before I saw
the Ocean river and the sharks hanging
under the sargassum weed lines,
a blue river in green water,
and the sharks staring back, sinking

down listlessly into darker water;
the torpor of heat, a hundred low-tide
nights begging a forgetfulness
I haven't quite earned.

I forgot where I heard that poems
are designed to waken sleeping gods;
in our time they've taken on nearly
unrecognizable shapes as gods will do;
one is a dog, one is a scarecrow
that doesn't work – crows perch
on the wind-whipped sleeves,
one is a carpenter who doesn't become Jesus,
one is a girl who went to heaven
sixty years early. Gods die,
and not always out of choice,
like near-sighted cats jumping
between buildings seven stories up.
One god drew feathers out of my skin
so I could fly, a favor close to terror.
But this isn't a map of the gods.
When they live in rivers
it's because rivers have no equilibrium;
gods resent equilibrium when everything
that lives *moves*; boulders
are a war of atoms, and the dandelion
cracks upward through the blacktop road.
Seltzer's tropical beetle grew
from a larval lump in a man's arm,
emerging full grown, pincers waving.
On Mt. Cuchama there were so many

gods passing through I hid in a hole
in a rock, waking one by accident.
I fled with a tight ass and cold skin.
I could draw a map of this place
but they're never caught in the same location
twice. And their voices change from involuntary
screams to the singular wail of the loon,
possibly the wind that can howl down Wall St.
Gods have long abandoned the banality of war
though they were stirred by a hundred-year-old
guitarist I heard in Brazil, also the autistic child
at the piano. We'll be greeted at death
so why should I wait? Today I invoked
any available god back in the woods in the fog.
The world was white with last week's melting
blizzard, the fog drifting upward, then descending.
The only sound was a porcupine eating bark
off an old tree, and a rivulet beneath the snow.
Sometimes the obvious is true: the full
moon on her bare bottom by the river!
For the gay, the full moon on the lover's prick!
Gods laugh at the fiction of gender.
Water-gods, moon-gods, god-fever,
sun-gods, fire-gods, give this earth-diver
more songs before I die.

A "system" suggests the cutting off,
i.e., in channel morphology, the reduction,
the suppression of texture to simplify:
to understand a man, or woman, growing
old with eagerness you first consider

the sensuality of death, an unacknowledged
surprise to most. In nature the physiology
has heat and color, beast and tree
saying aloud the wonder of death;
to study rivers, including the postcard
waterfalls, is to adopt another life;
a limited life attaches itself to the endless
movement, the renowned underground
rivers of South America which I've felt
thundering far beneath my feet – to die
is to descend into such rivers and flow
along in the perfect dark. But above ground
I'm memorizing life, from the winter moon
to the sound of my exhaustion in March
when all the sodden plans have collapsed
and only daughters, the dogs and cats
keep one from disappearing at gunpoint.
I brought myself here and stare nose to nose
at the tolerant cat who laps whiskey
from my mustache. Life often shatters
in schizoid splinters. I will avoid
becoming the cold stone wall I am straddling.

I had forgot what it was I liked
about life. I hear if you own a chimpanzee
they cease at a point to be funny. Writers
and politicians share an embarrassed moment
when they are sure all problems will disappear
if you get the language right.
That's not all they share – in each other's
company they are like boys who have been

discovered at wiener-play in the toilet.
At worst, it's the gift of gab.
At best it's Martin Luther King and Rimbaud.
Bearing down hard on love and death
there is an equal and opposite reaction.
All these years they have split the pie,
leaving the topping for the preachers
who don't want folks to fuck or eat.
What kind of magic, or rite of fertility,
to transcend this shit-soaked stew?

The river is as far as I can move
from the world of numbers: I'm all
for full retreats, escapes, a 47 yr. old runaway.
"Gettin' too old to run away," I wrote
but not quite believing this option is gray.
I stare into the deepest pool of the river
which holds the mystery of a cellar to a child,
and think of those two-track roads that dwindle
into nothing in the forest. I have this feeling
of walking around for days with the wind
knocked out of me. In the cellar was a root
cellar where we stored potatoes, apples, carrots
and where a family of harmless blacksnakes lived.
In certain rivers there are pools a hundred
foot deep. In a swamp I must keep secret
there is a deep boiling spring around which
in the dog days of August large brook trout
swim and feed. An adult can speak dreams
to children saying that there is a spring
that goes down to the center of the earth.

Maybe there is. Next summer I'm designing
and building a small river about seventy-seven
foot long. It will flow both ways, in reverse
of nature. I will build a dam and blow it up.

The involuntary image that sweeps
into the mind, irresistible and without evident
cause as a dream or thunderstorm,
or rising to the surface from childhood,
the longest journey taken in a split second,
from there to now, without pause:
in the woods with Mary Cooper, my first love
wearing a violet scarf in May. We're
looking after her huge mongoloid aunt,
trailing after this woman who loves us
but so dimly perceives the world. We pick
and clean wild leeks for her. The creek
is wild and dangerous with the last
of the snowmelt. The child–woman
tries to enter the creek and we tackle her.
She's stronger, then slowly understands,
half-wet and muddy. She kisses me
while Mary laughs, then Mary kisses me
over and over. Now I see the pools
in the Mongol eyes that watch and smile
with delight and hear the roar of the creek,
smell the scent of leeks on her muddy lips.

This is an obscene koan set plumb
in the middle of the Occident:
the man with three hands lacks symmetry

but claps the loudest, the chicken
in circles on the sideless road, a plane
that takes off and can never land.
I am not quite alert enough to live.
The fallen nest and fire in the closet,
my world without guardrails, the electric
noose, the puddle that had no bottom.
The fish in underground rivers are white
and blind as the porpoises who live far up
the muddy Amazon. In New York and LA
you don't want to see, hear, smell,
and you only open your mouth in restaurants.
At night you touch people with rock-hard skins.
I'm trying to become alert enough to live.
Yesterday after the blizzard I hiked far back
in a new swamp and found an iceless
pond connected to the river by a small creek.
Against deep white snow and black trees
there was a sulfurous fumarole, rank and sharp
in cold air. The water bubbled up brown,
then spread in turquoise to deep black,
without the track of a single mammal to drink.
This was nature's own, a beauty too strong
for life; a place to drown not live.

On waking after the accident
I was presented with the "whole picture"
as they say, magnificently detailed,
a child's diorama of what life appears to be:
staring at the picture I became drowsy
with relief when I noticed a yellow

dot of light in the lower right-hand corner.
I unhooked the machines and tubes and crawled
to the picture, with an eyeball to the dot
of light, which turned out to be a miniature
tunnel at the end of which I could see
mountains and stars whirling and tumbling,
sheets of emotions, vertical rivers, upside-
down lakes, herds of unknown mammals, birds
shedding feathers and regrowing them instantly,
snakes with feathered heads eating their own
shed skins, fish swimming straight up,
the bottom of Isaiah's robe, live whales
on dry ground, lions drinking from a golden
bowl of milk, the rush of night,
and somewhere in this the murmur of gods –
a tree-rubbing-tree music, a sweet howl
of water and rock-grating-rock, fire
hissing from fissures, the moon settled
comfortably on the ground, beginning to roll.

KOBUN

Hotei didn't need a *zafu*,
saying that his ass was sufficient.
The head's a cloud anchor
that the feet must follow.
Travel light, he said,
or don't travel at all.

LOOKING FORWARD TO AGE

I will walk down to a marina
on a hot day and not go out to sea.

I will go to bed and get up early,
and carry too much cash in my wallet.

On Memorial Day I will visit the graves
of all those who died in my novels.

If I have become famous I'll wear a green
janitor's suit and row a wooden boat.

From a key ring on my belt will hang
thirty-three keys that open no doors.

Perhaps I'll take all of my grandchildren
to Disneyland in a camper but probably not.

One day standing in a river with my fly rod
I'll have the courage to admit my life.

In a one-room cabin at night I'll consign
photos, all tentative memories to the fire.

And you my loves, few as there have been, let's lie
and say it could never have been otherwise.

So that: we may glide off in peace, not howling
like orphans in this endless century of war.

HOMILY

These simple rules to live within – a black
pen at night, a gold pen in daylight,
avoid blue food and ten-ounce shots
of whiskey, don't point a gun at yourself,
don't snipe with the cri-cri-cri of a *becassine,*
don't use gas for starter fluid, don't read
dirty magazines in front of stewardesses –
it happens all the time; it's time to stop
cleaning your plate, forget the birthdays
of the dead, give all you can to the poor.
This might go on and on and will: who can
choose between the animal in the road
and the ditch? A magnum for lunch
is a little too much but not enough
for dinner. Polish the actual stars at night
as an invisible man pets a dog, an actual
man a memory-dog lost under
the morning glory trellis forty years ago.
Dance with yourself with all your heart
and soul, and occasionally others, but don't
eat all the berries birds eat or you'll die.
Kiss yourself in the mirror but don't fall in love
with photos of ladies in magazines. Don't fall
in love as if you were falling through
the floor in an abandoned house, or off
a dock at night, or down a crevasse
covered with false snow, a cow floundering
in quicksand while the other cows watch
without particular interest, backward
off a crumbling cornice. Don't fall in love
with two at once. From the ceiling you can see

this circle of three, though one might be elsewhere.
He is rended, he rends himself, he dances,
he whirls so hard everything he *is* flies off.
He crumples as paper but rises daily from the dead.

SOUTHERN CROSS

That hot desert beach in Ecuador,
with scarcely a splotch of vegetation
fronting as it does
a Pacific so immensely lush
it hurls lobsters on great flat
boulders where children brave fatal
waves to pick them up.
Turning from one to the other quickly,
it is incomprehensible: from wild, gray
sunblasted burro eating cactus to azure
immensity of ocean, from miniature
goat dead on infantile feet in sand
to imponderable roar of swells, equatorial sun;
music that squeezes the blood out of the heart
by midnight, and girls whose legs
glisten with sweat, their teeth white
as Canadian snow, legs pounding as plump
brown pistons, and night noises I've
never heard, though at the coolest period
in these latitudes, near the faintest
beginning of dawn, there was the cold
unmistakable machine gun, the harshest
chatter death can make. Only then do
I think of my very distant relative, Lorca,
that precocious skeleton, as he crumpled
earthward against brown pine needles;
and the sky, vaster than the Pacific,
whirled overhead, a sky without birds or clouds,
azul te quiero azul.

SULLIVAN POEM

March 5: first day without a fire.
Too early. Too early. Too early!
Take joy in the day
without consideration, the three
newly-brought-to-life bugs
who are not meant to know
what they are doing avoid each other
on windows stained
by a dozen storms.

We eat our father's food:
herring, beans, salt pork,
sauerkraut, pig hocks, salt cod.
I have said good-bye with one thousand
laments so that even the heart of the rose
becomes empty as my dog's rubber ball.
The dead are not meant to go,
but to trail off so that one can
see them on a distant hillock,
across the river, in dreams
from which one awakens nearly healed:
don't worry, it's fine to be dead,
they say; we were a little early
but could not help ourselves.
Everyone dies as the child they were,
and at the moment, this secret,
intricately concealed heart blooms
forth with the first song anyone
sang in the dark, "Now I lay me
down to sleep, I pray the Lord
my soul to keep…"

Now this oddly gentle winter, almost dulcet,
winds to a blurred close with trees full
of birds that belong farther south,
and people are missing something
to complain about; a violent March
is an unacknowledged prayer;
a rape of nature, a healing blizzard,
a very near disaster.

So this last lament:
as unknowable as the eye of the crow
staring down from the walnut tree,
blind as the Magellanic clouds,
as cold as that March mud puddle
at the foot of the granary steps,
unseeable as the birthright of the LA
whore's Nebraska childhood of lilacs
and cornfields and an unnamed prairie
bird that lived in a thicket
where she hid,
as treacherous as a pond's spring
ice to a child,
black as the scar of a half-peeled
birch tree,
the wrench of the beast's heart just
short of the waterhole,
as bell-clear as a gunshot at dawn,
is the ache of a father's death.

It is that, but far more:
as if we take a voyage out of life

as surely as we took a voyage in,
almost as frightened children
in a cellar's cold gray air;
or before memory – they put me on a boat
on this river, then I was lifted off;
in our hearts, it is always just after
dawn, and each bird's song is the first,
and that ever-so-slight breeze that touches
the tops of trees and ripples the lake
moves through our bodies as if we were gods.

HORSE

What if it were our privilege
to sculpt our dreams of animals?
But those shapes in the night
come and go too quickly to be held
in stone: but not to avoid these shapes
as if dreams were only a nighttime
pocket to be remembered and avoided.
Who can say in the depths of
his life and heart what beast
most stopped life, the animals
he watched, the animals he only touched
in dreams? Even our hearts don't beat
the way we want them to. What
can we know in that waking,
sleeping edge? We put down
my daughter's old horse, old and
arthritic, a home burial. By dawn with eye
half-open, I said to myself, is
he still running, is he still running
around, under the ground?

COBRA

What are these nightmares,
so wildly colored? We're in every
movie we see, even in our sleep.
Not that we can become what
we fear most but that we can't
resist ourselves. The grizzly
attack; after that divorce
and standing outside the school
with a rifle so they can't take my
daughter Anna. By god! Long ago
in Kenya where I examined the
grass closely before I sat down
to a poisonous lunch, I worried
about cobras. When going insane I worried
about cobra venom in Major Grey's Chutney.
Simple as that. Then in overnight sleep I became
a lordly cobra, feeling the pasture grass
at high noon glide beneath my
stomach. I watched the house with
my head arched above the weeds,
then slept in the cool dirt under the granary.

PORPOISE

Every year, when we're fly-fishing for tarpon
off Key West, Guy insists that porpoises
are good luck. But it's not so banal
as catching more fish or having a fashion
model fall out of the sky lightly on your head,
or at your feet depending on certain
preferences. It's what porpoises do to the ocean.
You see a school making love off Boca Grande,
the baby with his question mark staring
at us a few feet from the boat.
Porpoises dance for as long as they live.
You can do nothing for them.
They alter the universe.

THE BRAND NEW STATUE OF LIBERTY

to Lee Iacocca (another Michigan boy)

I was commissioned in a dream by Imanja,
also the Black Pope of Brazil, Tancred,
to design a seven-tiered necklace
of seven thousand skulls for the Statue of Liberty.
Of course from a distance they'll look
like pearls, but in November
when the strongest winds blow, the skulls
will rattle wildly, bone against metal,
a crack and chatter of bone against metal,
the true sound of history, this metal striking bone.
I'm not going to get heavy-handed –
a job is a job and I've leased a football
field for the summer, gathered a group of ladies
who are art lovers, leased in advance
a bull Sikorsky freight helicopter
to drop on the necklace: funding comes
from Ford Foundation, Rockefeller, the NEA.
There is one Jewish skull from Atlanta, two
from Mississippi, but this is basically
an indigenous cast except skulls from tribes
of blacks who got a free ride over from Africa,
representative skulls from all the Indian
tribes, an assortment of grizzly, wolf,
coyote and buffalo skulls. But what beauty
when the morning summer sun glances
off these bony pates! And her great
iron lips quivering in a smile, almost a smirk
so that she'll drop the torch to fondle the jewels.

THE TIMES ATLAS

For my mentor, long dead, Richard Halliburton
and his Seven League Boots.

Today was the coldest day in the history
of the Midwest. Thank god for the moon
in this terrible storm.

There are areas far out at sea where
it rains a great deal. Camus said
it rained so hard even the sea was wet.

O god all our continents are only rifted
magma welled up from below. We don't
have a solid place to stand.

A little bullshit here as the Nile
is purportedly eighty miles longer
than the Amazon. I proclaim it a tie.

Pay out your 125 bucks and find out the world
isn't what you think it is but what
it is. We whirl so nothing falls off.
Eels, polar bears, bugs and men enjoy

the maker's design. No one really
leaves this place. O loveliness
of Caribbean sun off water under
trade wind's lilt.

Meanwhile the weather is no longer amusing.
Earth frightens me, the blizzard, house's
shudder, oceanic roar, the brittle night
that might leave so many dead.

NEW LOVE

With these dire portents
we'll learn the language
of knees, shoulder blades,
chins but not the first floor up,
shinbones, the incomprehensible
belly buttons of childhood,
heels and the soles of our feet,
spines and neckbones,
risqué photos of the tender
inside of elbows, tumescent fingers
draw the outlines of lost parts
on the wall; bottom and pubis
Delphic, unapproachable as Jupiter,
a memory worn as the first love
we knew, ourselves a test pattern
become obsession: this love
in the plague years – we used to kiss
a mirror to see if we were dead.
Now we relearn the future as we learned
to walk, as a baby grabs its toes,
tilts backward, rocking. Tonight I'll touch
your wrist and in a year perhaps grind
my blind eye's socket against your hipbone.
With all this death, behind our backs,
the moon has become the moon again.

WHAT HE SAID WHEN I WAS ELEVEN

August, a dense heat wave at the cabin
mixed with torrents of rain,
the two-tracks become miniature rivers.

In the Russian Orthodox Church
one does not talk to God, one sings.
This empty and sun-blasted land

has a voice rising in shimmers.
I did not sing in Moscow
but St. Basil's in Leningrad raised

a quiet tune. But now seven worlds
away I hang the *cazas-moscas*
from the ceiling and catch seven flies

in the first hour, buzzing madly
against the stickiness. I've never seen
the scissor-tailed flycatcher, a favorite

bird of my youth, the worn Audubon
card pinned to the wall. When I miss
flies three times with the swatter

they go free for good. Fair is fair.
There is too much nature pressing against
the window as if it were a green night;

and the river swirling in glazed turbulence
is less friendly than ever before.
Forty years ago she called, *Come home, come home,*

it's suppertime. I was fishing a fishless
cattle pond with a new three-dollar pole,
dreaming the dark blue ocean of pictures.

In the barn I threw down hay
while my Swede grandpa finished milking,
squirting the barn cat's mouth with an udder.

I kissed the wet nose of my favorite cow,
drank a dipper of fresh warm milk
and carried two pails to the house,

scraping the manure off my feet
in the pump shed. She poured the milk
in the cream separator and I began cranking.

At supper the oilcloth was decorated
with worn pink roses. We ate cold herring,
also the bluegills we had caught at daylight.

The fly-strip above the table idled in
the window's breeze, a new fly in its death buzz.
Grandpa said, "We are all flies."

That's what he said forty years ago.

ACTING

for J.N.

In the best sense,
becoming another
so that there is no trace left
of what we think is the self.
I am whoever.
It is not gesture
but the cortex of gesture,
not movement
but the soul of movement.
Look at the earth with your left eye
and at the sky with your right.
Worship contraries.
What makes us alike
is also what makes us different.
From Man to Jokester to Trickster
is a nudge toward the deep,
the incalculable abyss
you stare into so it will
stare back into you.
We are our consciousness
and it is the god in us
who struggles to be in everyone
in order to be ourselves.
When you see the chalked form
of the murdered man on the cement
throw yourself onto it and feel
the heat of the stone-hard fit.
This is the liquid poem,
the forefinger traced around both

the neck and the sun:
to be and be and be
as a creek turns corners
by grace of volume, heft of water,
speed by rate of drop,
even the contour of stone
changing day by day.
So that: when you wake in the night,
the freedom of the nightmare
turned to dream follows you
into morning, and there is no
skin on earth you cannot enter,
no beast or plant,
no man or woman
you may not flow through
and become.

MY FRIEND THE BEAR

Down in the bone myth of the cellar
of this farmhouse, behind the empty fruit jars
the whole wall swings open to the room
where I keep the bear. There's a tunnel
to the outside on the far wall that emerges
in the lilac grove in the backyard
but she rarely uses it, knowing there's no room
around here for a freewheeling bear.
She's not a dainty eater so once a day
I shovel shit while she lopes in playful circles.
Privately she likes religion – from the bedroom
I hear her incantatory moans and howls
below me – and April 23rd, when I open
the car trunk and whistle at midnight
and she shoots up the tunnel, almost airborne
when she meets the night. We head north
and her growls are less friendly as she scents
the forest-above-the-road smell. I release
her where I found her as an orphan three
years ago, bawling against the dead carcass
of her mother. I let her go at the head
of the gully leading down to the swamp,
jumping free of her snarls and roars.
But each October 9th, one day before bear season
she reappears at the cabin frightening
the bird dogs. We embrace ear to ear,
her huge head on my shoulder,
her breathing like god's.

CABIN POEM

I

The blond girl
with a polka heart:
one foot, then another,
then aerial
in a twisting jump,
chin upward
with a scream of such
splendor
I go back to my cabin,
and start a fire.

II

Art & life
drunk & sober
empty & full
guilt & grace
cabin & home
north & south
struggle & peace
after which we catch
a glimpse of stars,
the white glistening pelt
of the Milky Way,
hear the startled bear crashing
through the delta swamp below me.
In these troubled times
I go inside and start a fire.

III

I am the bird that hears the worm,
or, my cousin said, the pulse of a wound
that probes to the opposite side.
I have abandoned alcohol, cocaine,
the news, and outdoor prayer
as support systems.
How can you make a case for yourself
before an ocean of trees, or standing
waist-deep in the river? Or sitting
on the logjam with a pistol?
I reject oneness with bears.
She has two cubs and thinks she
owns the swamp I thought I bought.
I shoot once in the air to tell her
it's my turn at the logjam
for an hour's thought about nothing.
Perhaps that is oneness with bears.
I've decided to make up my mind
about nothing, to assume the water mask,
to finish my life disguised as a creek,
an eddy, joining at night the full,
sweet flow, to absorb the sky,
to swallow the heat and cold, the moon
and the stars, to swallow myself
in ceaseless flow.

RICH FOLKS, POOR FOLKS, AND NEITHER

I

Rich folks keep their teeth
until late in life,
and park their cars in heated garages.
They own kitsch statues of praying hands
that conceal seven pounds of solid gold,
knowing that burglars hedge at icons.
At the merest twinge they go to the dentist,
and their dogs' anuses are professionally
inspected for unsuspected diseases.
Rich folks dream of the perfect massage
that will bring secret, effortless orgasm,
and absolutely super and undiscovered
islands with first-rate hotels
where they will learn to windsurf
in five minutes. They buy clothes that fit –
a forty waist means forty pants – rich folks
don't squeeze into thirty-eights. At spas
they are not too critical of their big asses,
and they believe in real small portions
because they can eat again pretty quick.
Rich folks resent richer folks
and they also resent poor folks
for their failures at meniality.
It's unfortunate for our theory that the same
proportion of rich folks are as pleasant
as poor folks, a pitiless seven
percent, though not necessarily the ones
who still say their prayers and finish
the morning oatmeal to help the poor.

Everyone I have ever met is deeply
puzzled.

II

Up in Michigan poor folks dream of trips
to Hawaii or "Vegas." They muttered deeply
when the banker won the big lottery –
"It just don't seem fair," they said.
Long ago when I was poor
there was something in me that craved
to get fired, to drink a shot and beer
with a lump in my throat, hitchhike
or drive to California in an old car,
tell my family "I'll write if I get work."
In California, where you can sleep outside
every night, I saw the Pacific Ocean
and ate my first food of the Orient,
a fifty-cent bowl of noodles and pork.
No more cornmeal mush with salt pork
gravy, no more shovels at dawn,
no more clothes smelling of kerosene,
no more girls wearing ankle bracelets spelling
another's name. No more three-hour waits
in unemployment lines, or cafeteria catsup
and bread for fifteen cents. I've eaten
my last White Tower burger and I'm heading
for the top. Or not. How could I dream
I'd end up moist-eyed in the Beverly Hills Hotel
when I ordered thirteen appetizers for myself
and the wheels of the laden trolley squeaked?

The television in the limousine broke down
and I missed the news on the way to look
at the ocean where there were no waves.
When I went bankrupt I began to notice cemeteries
and wore out my clothes, drank up the wine cellar.
I went to the movies and kissed my wife a lot
for the same reason – they're both in technicolor.
Everyone I met in those days was deeply puzzled.

III

Now I've rubbed rich and poor together
like two grating stones, mixed them temporarily
like oil and vinegar, male and female, until
my interest has waned to nothing. One night I saw
a constellation that chose not to reappear,
drifting in the day into another galaxy.
I tried to ignore the sound of my footsteps
in the woods until I did, and when I swam
in the river I finally forgot it was water,
but I still can't see a cow without saying *cow*.
Perhaps this was not meant to be. I dug
a deep hole out in a clearing in the forest
and sat down in it, studying the map
of the sky above me for clues, a new bible.
This is rushing things a bit, I thought.
I became a woman then became a man again.
I hiked during the night alone and gave
my dogs fresh bones until they no longer cared.
I bought drinks for the poor and for myself,
left mail unopened, didn't speak on the phone,

only listened. I shot the copy machine with my rifle.
No more copies, I thought, everything original!
Now I am trying to unlearn the universe
in the usual increments of nights and days.
Time herself often visits in swirling but gentle clouds.
Way out there on the borders of my consciousness
I've caught glimpses of that great dark bird,
the beating of whose wings is death, drawing closer.
How could it be otherwise? I thought.
Down in the hole last August during a thunderstorm
I watched her left wing-tip shudder past
between two lightning strokes. Maybe I'll see her again
during the northern lights, but then, at that moment,
I was still a child of water and mud.

DANCING

After the passing of irresistible
music you must learn to make
do with a dripping faucet,
rain or sleet on the roof,
eventually snow,
a cat's sigh,
the spherical notes that float
down from Aldebaran,
your cells as they part,
craving oxygen.

THE IDEA OF BALANCE IS TO BE FOUND IN HERONS AND LOONS

I just heard a loon-call on a TV ad
and my body gave itself
a quite voluntary shudder,
as in the night in East Africa
I heard the immense barking cough
of a lion, so foreign and indifferent.

But the lion drifts away
and the loon stays close,
calling, as she did in my childhood,
in the cold rain a song
that tells the world of men
to keep its distance.

It isn't the signal of another life
or the reminder of anything
except her call: still,
at this quiet point past midnight
the rain is the same rain
that fell so long ago, and the loon
says I'm seven years old again.

At the far ends of the lake
where no one lives or visits —
there are no roads to get there;
you take the watercourse way,
the quiet drip and drizzle
of oars, slight squeak of oarlock,
the bare feet can feel the cold water
move beneath the old wood boat.

At one end the lordly great blue herons
nest at the top of the white pine;
at the other end the loons,
just after daylight in cream-colored mist,
drifting with wails that begin as querulous,
rising then into the spheres in volume,
with lost or doomed angels imprisoned
within their breasts.

SMALL POEM

There's something I've never known
when I get up in the morning.
Dead children fly off in the shape
of question marks, the doe's backward
glance at the stillborn fawn.
I don't know what it is
in the morning, as if incomprehension
beds down with me on waking.
What is the precise emotional temperature
when the young man hangs himself
in the jail cell with his father's belt?
What is the foot size of the Beast of Belsen?
This man in his overremembered life
needs to know the source of the ache
which is an answer without a question,
his fingers wrapped around the memory
of life, as Cleopatra's around the snake's neck,
a shepherd's crook of love.

COUNTING BIRDS

for Gerald Vizenor

As a child, fresh out of the hospital
with tape covering the left side
of my face, I began to count birds.
At age fifty the sum total is precise
and astonishing, my only secret.
Some men count women or the cars
they've owned, their shirts –
long sleeved and short sleeved –
or shoes, but I have my birds,
excluding, of course, those extraordinary
days: the twenty-one thousand
snow geese and sandhill cranes at
Bosque del Apache; the sky blinded
by great frigate birds in the Pacific
off Anconcito, Ecuador; the twenty-one
thousand pink flamingos in Ngorongoro Crater
in Tanzania; the vast flock of seabirds
on the Seri coast of the Sea of Cortez
down in Sonora that left at nightfall,
then reappeared, resuming
their exact positions at dawn;
the one thousand cliff swallows nesting
in the sand cliffs of Pyramid Point,
their small round burrows like eyes,
really the souls of the Anasazi who flew
here a thousand years ago
to wait the coming of the Manitou.
And then there were the usual, almost deadly
birds of the soul – the crow with silver

harness I rode one night as if she
were a black, feathered angel;
the birds I became to escape unfortunate
circumstances – how the skin ached
as the feathers shot out toward light;
the thousand birds the dogs helped
me shoot to become a bird (grouse, woodcock,
duck, dove, snipe, pheasant, prairie chicken, etc.).
On my deathbed I'll write this secret
number on a slip of paper and pass
it to my wife and two daughters.
It will be a hot evening in late June
and they might be glancing out the window
at the thunderstorm's approach from the west.
Looking past their eyes and a dead fly
on the window screen I'll wonder
if there's a bird waiting for me in the onrushing clouds.
O birds, I'll sing to myself, *you've carried*
me along on this bloody voyage,
carry me now into that cloud,
into the marvel of this final night.

AFTER IKKYŪ
& OTHER POEMS

for Jack Turner

1996

PREFACE

I began my Zen studies and practice well over twenty years ago in a state of rapacious and self-congratulatory spiritual greed. I immediately set about reading hundreds of books on the subject, almost all contemporary and informed by an earnest mediocrity. There was no more self-referential organism alive than myself, a potato that didn't know it was a potato.

Naturally the years have passed quickly, if not brutishly. I practiced because I value life and this seems the best way for me to get at the heart of the matter. We are more than dying flies in a shithouse, though we are that, too. There are hundreds of ways to tip off a cushion and only one way to sit there. Zen is the vehicle of reality, and I see almost as much of it in Wordsworth as I do in Ch'an texts. As I've said before, it's easy to mistake the plumbing for the river. We in the West are prone to ignore our own literary traditions, while in the East Zennists were industriously syncretic, gathering poetry, Confucius, and Taoism to their breasts. There is scarcely a better koan than Ahab before the whiteness of a whale who sees a different ocean from each side of its massive head.

The sequence "After Ikkyū" was occasioned when Jack Turner passed along to me *The Record of Tung-shan* and the new *Master Yunmen,* edited by Urs App. It was a dark period, and I spent a great deal of time with the books. They rattled me loose from the oppressive, poleaxed state of distraction we count as worldly success. But then we are not fueled by piths and gists but by practice – which is Yunmen's unshakable point, amongst a thousand other harrowing ones. I was born a baby, what are these hundred suits of clothes I'm wearing?

Of course, the reader should be mindful that I'm a poet and we tend to err on the side that life is more than it appears rather than less. I do not remotely consider myself a "Zen Buddhist," as that is too ineptly convenient, and a specific barrier for one whose lifelong obsession has been his art rather than his religion. Someone like Robert Aitken Roshi is a Zen Buddhist. I'm still a fool. Early on in my teens I suffocated myself with Protestant theology and am mindful, in Coleridge's terms, that, like spiders, we spin webs of deceit out of our big hanging asses, whether with Jesus or the Buddha.

But still practice is accretive, and who has opened doors for me like Zen creatures – Peter Matthiessen, Gary Snyder, Kobun Chino Sensei, Bob Watkins, Dan Gerber, and Jack Turner, to name a few prominent ones?

It doesn't really matter if these poems are thought of as slightly soiled dharma gates or just plain poems. They'll live or die by their own specific density, flowers for the void. The poems were written within the discreet interval described so poignantly by Tung-shan:

> Earnestly avoid seeking without,
> Lest it recede far from you.
> Today I am walking alone,
> Yet everywhere I meet him.
> He is now no other than myself,
> But I am not now him.
> It must be understood this way
> In order to merge with Suchness.

To write a poem you must first create a pen that will write what you want to say. For better or worse, this is the work of a lifetime.

–J.H.
1996

AFTER IKKYŪ

1

Our minds buzz like bees
but not the bees' minds.
It's just wings not heart
they say, moving to another flower.

2

The well pit is beneath where the pump shed burned
years ago with a living roar, a fire lion. Down
in the pit, charred timbers, green grass, one burdock,
a vernal pool where frogs live trapped in a universe.

3

I've wasted too much moonlight.
Breast-beating. I'll waste no more moonlight,
the moon bullied by clouds drifts west
in her imponderable arc, snared for a half
hour among the wet leaves in the birdbath.

4

After thirty years of work
I take three months off
and wait for the mirror's image to fade.
These chess pieces, slippery with blood.

5

Time eats us alive.
On my birthday yesterday
I was only one day older
though I began ten million eons ago
as a single cell in the old mud homestead.

6

Shoju sat all night in the graveyard
among wolves who sniffed his Adam's apple.
First light moving in the air
he arose, peed, and ate breakfast.

7

With each shot
he killed the self
until there was no one left
to bring home the bacon.

8

One part of the brain attacks another,
seven parts attack nine parts,
then the war begins to subside
from lack of ammunition,
but out there I know the mules are bringing
fresh supplies from over the mountain.

9

Poor little blind boy lost in the storm,
where should he go to be without harm?
For starters, the dickhead should get a life.
Once I had a moment of absolute balance
while dancing with my sick infant daughter
to Merle Haggard. The blind boy died in the storm
with fresh frozen laughter hot on his lips.

10

Our pup is gravely ill.
She's her own pup too,
first in her own line.
How great thou art o god,
save her, please, the same cry
in every throat. May I live forever.

11

At Hard Luck Ranch the tea is hot,
the sky's dark blue. Behind me
the jaguar skin from the jaguar
who died so long ago from a bullet
while perched on a calf's back
tells me the same old story.

12

Not here and now but now and here.
If you don't know the difference
is a matter of life and death, get down
naked on bare knees in the snow
and study the ticking of your watch.

13

The hound I've known for three years
trots down the mountain road
with a nod at me, pretending he knows
what he's doing miles from home
on a sunlit morning. He's headed
for a kind of place he hasn't quite found yet
and might not recognize when he gets there.

14

At the strip club in Lincoln, Nebraska,
she said, "I'm the Princess of Shalimar."
Doubtless, I thought, at a loss for words
but not images, the air moist but without
the promise of a rain. She's not bending
pinkly like a pretzel but a body.
At this age, my first bona fide royalty.

15

Way up a sandy draw in the foothills
of the Whetstone Mountains I found cougar
tracks so fresh, damp sand was still
trickling in from the edges. For some reason
I knelt and sniffed them, quite sure
I was being watched by a living rock
in the vast, heat-blurred landscape.

16

I went to Tucson and it gave
me a headache. I don't know how.
Everyone's a cousin in this world.
I drove down a road of enormous houses
that encompass many toilets. Down hallways,
leaping left or right, you can crap at will.
A mile away a dead Mexican child slept
out in the desert on the wrong side of a mattress.

17

Up at the Hard Luck Ranch
there's a pyracantha bush full of red berries
right outside my study window.
In December after seven hard frosts
the birds arrive to eat the fermented berries.
The birds get drunk and unwary in this saloon
and the barn cats have a bird feast.
A phainopepla landed on my head, shrieking
when my eyebrow moved, booze on its bird breath.

18

My *zabuton* doubles as a dog bed. Rose sleeps
there, full to the fur with *mu*. Glanced in
on a moonlit night; her slight white figure coiled
on the green cushion, shaking with quail dreams.
Sensing me, an eye opens, single tail-wag. Back to sleep.
When she's awake, she's so awake I'm ashamed
of my own warm water dance, my sitting too long at the fire.

19

Time gets foreshortened late at night.
Jesus died a few days ago, my father
and sister just before lunch. At dawn
I fished, then hoed corn. Married at midmorning,
wept for a second. We were poor momentarily
for a decade. Within a few minutes I made
a round trip to Paris. I drank and ate during a parade
in my room. One blink, Red Mountain's still there.

20

More lion prints in our creek bed.
Right now in the light cool rain at midnight,
coyotes. Skunk stink laden in the mist.
Hidden moon, I don't want to go home yet.
Older, the flavors of earth are more delicious.

21

Just like today eternity is accomplished
in split seconds. I read that Old Nieh
in the wilderness vastness trained a mountain
tiger to carry his firewood. A black hole the size
of 300 billion suns is gobbling up the M87
galaxy because astronomers gave it a boring name.
Time passed in sitting begs mercy from the clock.

22

Out in an oak-lined field down the road
I again saw time, trotting in circles
around the far edges. The dog didn't notice
though she's usually more attentive. She lost
the Christmas watch I gave her
in a mountain canyon at the edge of earth.

23

It certainly wasn't fish who discovered water
or birds the air. Men built houses in part
out of embarrassment by the stars
and raised their children on trivialities
because they had butchered the god within themselves.
The politician standing on the church steps thrives
within the grandeur of this stupidity,
a burnt-out lamp who never imagined the sun.

24

The monk is eighty-seven. There's no fat
left on his feet to defend against stones.
He forgot his hat, larger in recent years.
By a creek he sees a woman he saw fifty summers
before, somehow still a girl to him. Once again his hands
tremble when she gives him a tin cup of water.

25

Talked to the God of Hosts about the Native American
situation and he said everything's a matter of time,
that though it's small comfort the ghosts have already
nearly destroyed us with the ugliness we've become,
that in a few hidden glades in North America
half-human bears still dance in imperfect circles.

26

This adobe is no protection against the flossy
sweep of stars that in recent nights burn pinprick
holes in my skin, mostly in the skull despite my orange
stocking cap, hunter's orange so you won't get shot
by other hunters, a color the stars readily ignore
with beams of white fire. O stars, you forsaken suns.

27

I confess that here and there in my life
there is a vision of a great brown toad
leaking words of love and doom through his skin,

excrescences that would kill anyone, given time,
his words tinged as they are with the shapes
of death, one drumbeat, a heartbeat, the skins
of gods a rug spread beneath our feet.

28

Lin-chi says, having thrown away your head so long
ago, you go on and on looking for it in the wrong
places. The head's future can be studied in a spadeful
of dirt. The delightful girl I loved 40 years back
now weighs, according to necrologists, 30 lbs. net.
Why does she still swim in the eddy in the river's bend?

29

The four seasons, the ten oaths, the nine colors, three vowels
that stretch forth their paltry hands to the seven flavors
and the one money, the official parody of prayer.
Up on this mountain, stumbling on talus, on the north face
there is snow, and on the south, buds of pink flowers.

30

It is difficult to imagine the wordless conversations
between Jesus and Buddha going on this very moment.
These androgynous blood brothers demand our imagination.
They could ask Shakespeare and Mozart to write words
and music, and perhaps a dozen others, but they've done so.
The vast asteroid on its way toward LA goes unmentioned.

31

Come down to earth! Get your head out of your ass!
Get your head out of the clouds! Stop mooning around!
Pay attention. Get to work on time.
Time and tide that wait for no man willingly
pause for the barearmed girl brushing her hair
in a brown pickup truck on a summer evening.

32

If that bald head gets you closer to Buddha
try chemotherapy. Your hair drops casually to the floor,
eyes widen until the skull aches, the heart beats like
Thumper's foot. Heaven's near at every second.
Now you've become that lamb you refused to eat.

33

I haven't accepted the fact that I'll never understand
the universe that I saw clearly for the first time
from our roof at nineteen in miniature *kensho*.
We belonged to each other. Love at first sight,
notwithstanding the child who stared in fear
at the northern lights and noted the Milky Way's convulsive
drift. A lone star perched on the mountain's
saddle now brings tears of doubt.

34

It wasn't until the sixth century that the Christians
decided animals weren't part of the kingdom of heaven.
Hoof, wing, and paw can't put money in the collection plate.
These lunatic shit-brained fools excluded our beloved creatures.
Theologians and accountants, the same thing really, join
evangelists on television, shadowy as viruses.

35

Everywhere I go I study the scars on earth's face,
including rivers and lakes. I'm not playing God
but assessing intent. In the Patagonia Mountains
you think, "small mines, pathetic deaths." In Cabeza Prieta
men boiled in their own blood, ground temperature 170°F.
Contrails of earthen scar-tissue stink of sulfur.
Gold & copper to buy the horse that died, the woman who left.

36

Ten thousand pointless equations left just after dawn,
the city's air heavy with the fat of countless dieters.
Saw Ummon strolling down Wilshire with Yunmen,
unperturbed, disappearing into each other, emerging
with laughter. Saw thirty-three green, waking parrots
watch a single black cat raising the dew as she walked
across the golf course, the first one to the seventh tee.

37

Beware, o wanderer, the road is walking too,
said Rilke one day to no one in particular
as good poets everywhere address the six directions.
If you can't bow, you're dead meat. You'll break
like uncooked spaghetti. Listen to the gods.
They're shouting in your ear every second.

38

Who remembers Wang Chi, "the real human like
multiplied sunlight"? No one, of course,
but his words are a lamp for any fool's feet.
He can't stop you from drowning, but he can keep
you out of the boat. This water's meant for careful wading,
but imagining my ears are gills, I still dive there at night.

39

In the next installment I'll give you Crazy Horse and Anne Frank,
their conversation as recorded by Matthew of Gospel fame,
who was wont, as all scriveners, to add a bit of this and that.
God is terse. The earth's proper scripture could be carried
on a three-by-five card if we weren't drunk on our own blood.

40

Walking the lakeshore at first moonlight I can see
feathers, stones, smooth spars, seaweed,
and the doe washed up from the Manitous two days ago

has been nearly eaten by the coyotes and ravens.   ,
I poke my stick in the moon's watery face, then apologize.

41

Home again. It looked different for a moment.
The birds, while not decrepit, flew slower.
The dogs wagged and licked their greetings,
then went back to sleep, unmindful of airplanes.
The new moon said either gather yourself for your last
decade, or slow down big pony, fat snake shed another skin.

42

Inside people fear the outside; outside, the in.
But then I'm always halfway in or out the door,
most comfortable and at home in this fear,
knowing that falling is best for my nature.
Backward works well, or gathered for the leeward
pitch, imitate the sea in perfect balance in her torment.

43

The world is wrenched on her pivot, shivering. Politicians
and preachers are standing on their heads, shitting
out of their mouths. Lucky for us Stephen Mitchell
has restored the Gospels, returning the Jesus
I imagined at fourteen, offering up my clumsy life
in a damp shroud of hormones. Most of all he said,
"Pay attention" – Buddha nodding from the wings.

44

The dawn of the day we arrived, Abel Murrietta
saw a big mountain lion sitting behind our gate.
This is not an omen but a lion, the border guard
athwart our time in the chaos of the wild, the other
that draws us to speechlessness, the lion behind the gate
turning her head, flowing up the mountainside to sit,
gazing at twilight at the *casita,* creek bed, our shared thickets.

45

The sound of the dog's pawsteps move away
at the precise speed of his shadow. Nothing is blurred.
The bullet tumbled toward the girl's head at 1250 feet
per second. She wasn't the president, you say,
too young for politics. Despite theological gooseshit
the gods don't keep time in light-years. We're slowed
to the brutality of clocks. Listen to the alarm. Wake up.

46

Sometimes a toothpick is the most important thing;
others, a roll of toilet paper. If you forget red wine
and garlic you'll become honky new-age incense
dressed in invisible taffeta. Eat meat or not,
try weighing your virtue on that bathroom scale
right after you crap and shower. You're just a tree
that grows shit, not fruit. Your high horse is dead meat.

47

The girl's bottom is beautiful as Peacock's dancing bear
who is 70 miles from any of our fevered instruments.
Neither girl nor bear utter a word to the world in between
in its careless sump. The Virgin said zip to the Garrison.
If you can't dance without music jump into an icy lake.
Think of the brown girl at the A&W Root Beer stand.

48

It was Monday morning for most of the world
and my heart nearly exploded according
to my digital high-blood-pressure machine,
telling me I don't want to work anymore
as the highest-paid coal miner on earth.
I want to stay up on the surface and help the heron
who's been having trouble with his creek-bed landings.
He's getting old and I wonder where he'll be when he dies.

49

Jesus wants me for a sunbeam, I sang in Sunday
school a lifetime ago, way up in cold country
where there wasn't much sun. A sunbeam in winter
made one recoil, and everyone stared mutely upward.
The bogeyman still smiles, now from a glass
of whiskey, then from a farmhouse root cellar.
A little boy bred this man with no thought of the future.

50

If I'm not mistaken, everyone seems to go back
to where they came from, ending up right
where they began. Our beloved cat died today.
She liked to sit on my head during *zazen*
back when she was a child. I bow to her magnificence
beside which all churches and temples are privy holes.

51

A lovely woman in Minnesota owned a 100-year-old horse,
actually thirty-seven, but in horse years that's at least 100.
In the third grade I read there were eleven surviving
Civil War veterans. Under the photo captions it said
they were mostly drummer boys. Now both
horse and veterans are dead, the woman married, rid
of her binding sweetheart horse. I know these peculiar
things because I'm Jim, at the right place, the right time.

52

Once and for all there's no genetic virtue.
Our cherubic baldy flounces around, fresh out of Boulder,
in black robes, Japanese words quick on his tongue.
World War II nearly destroyed my family, so I ask
him to learn Chinese. He understands I'm a fool.
Then over a gallon of wine we agree there's no language
for such matters, no happiness outside consciousness. Drink.

53

Sam got tired of the way life fudged the big issues,
drank a quart of vodka, shot himself in the parking lot
of the tavern. How could a friend do this to himself?
It was relatively easy. Anyone can do it in a blink.
We won't look for black bears again out by Barfield Lakes.
Some don't go up in smoke but are strangled off the earth.

54

This morning I felt strong and jaunty in my mail-order
Israeli commando trousers. Up at Hard Luck Ranch I spoke
to the ravens in baritone, fed the cats with manly gestures.
Acacia thorns can't penetrate these mighty pants. Then out
by the corral the infant pup began to weep, abandoned.
In an instant I became another of earth's billion sad mothers.

55

I once thought that life's what's left over after
I extricate myself from the mess. I was writing a poem
about paying attention and microwaved a hot dog
so hot it burned a beet-red hole in the roof of my mouth.
Lucrezia Borgia got shit on her fingers by not paying
attention. Chanting a sutra, the monk stepped fatally
on the viper's tail. Every gun is loaded and cocked.

56

I've emerged from the seven-going-on-eight divorces
that have surrounded me for three years. I kept on saying
look at me, I'm not wise. I've advised seven suicides.
No one's separate. Our legs grow into the horse's body.
You've ridden each other too long to get off now.
You can make a clean getaway only if you cut off your heads.
All in vain. Life won't get simple until our minds do.
Embrace the great emptiness; say again, I don't do divorces.

57

Took my own life because I was permanently crippled,
put on backward, the repairs eating up money and time.
For fifty-seven years I've had it all wrong
until I studied the other side of the mirror.
No birth before death. The other way around.
How pleasant to get off a horse in the middle of the lake.

THE DAVENPORT LUNAR ECLIPSE

Overlooking the Mississippi
I never thought I'd get this old.
It was mostly my confusion about time
and the moon, and seeing the lovely way
homely old men treat their homely old women
in Nebraska and Iowa, the lunch time
touch over green Jell-O with pineapple
and fried "fish rectangles" for $2.95.
When I passed Des Moines the radio said
there were long lines to see the entire cow
sculpted out of butter. The earth is right smack
between the sun and the moon, the black waitress
told me at the Salty Pelican on the waterfront,
home from wild Houston to nurse her sick dad.
My good eye is burning up from fatigue
as it squints up above the Mississippi
where the moon is losing its edge to black.
It likely doesn't know what's happening to it,
I thought, pressed down to my meal and wine
by a fresh load of incomprehension.
My grandma lived in Davenport in the 1890s
just after Wounded Knee, a signal event,
the beginning of America's *Sickness unto Death*.
I'd like to nurse my father back to health
he's been dead thirty years, I said
to the waitress who agreed. That's why she
came home, she said, you only got one.
Now I find myself at fifty-one in Davenport
and drop the issue right into the Mississippi
where it is free to swim with the moon's reflection.
At the bar there are two girls of incomprehensible beauty

for the time being, as Swedish as my Grandma,
speaking in bad grammar as they listen to a band
of middle-aged Swede saxophonists braying
"Bye-Bye Blackbird" over and over, with a clumsy
but specific charm. The girls fail to notice me –
perhaps I should give them the thousand dollars
in my wallet but I've forgotten just how.
I feel pleasantly old and stupid, deciding
not to worry about who I am but how I spend
my days, until I tear in the weak places
like a thin, worn sheet. Back in my room
I can't hear the river passing like time,
or the moon emerging from the shadow of earth,
but I can see the water that never repeats itself.
It's very difficult to look at the World
and into your heart at the same time.
In between, a life has passed.

COYOTE NO. I

Just before dark
watched coyote take a crap
on rock outcropping,
flexing hips (no time off)
swiveled owl-like to see
in all six directions:
sky above
earth below,
points of compass
in two half-circles.
There.
And there is no distance.
He knows the dreamer
that dreams his dreams.

TIME SUITE

Just seven weeks ago in Paris
I read Chuang Tzu in my dreams
and remembered once again
we are only here for a moment,
not very wild mushrooms,
just cartoon creatures that are blown apart
and only think they are put back together,
housepets within a house fire of impermanence.
In this cold cellar we see light
without knowing it is out of reach;
not to be owned but earned
moment by moment.
But still at dawn
in the middle of Paris's heart
there was a crow I spoke to
on the cornice far above my window.
It is the crow from home
that cawed above the immense
gaunt bear eating sweet-pea vines
and wild strawberries.
Today in the garden of Luxembourg
I passed through clumps of frozen vines
and saw a man in a bulletproof
glass house guarding stone,
a girl in the pink suit
of an unknown animal,
lovers nursing at each other's mouths.
I know that at my deathbed's urging
there'll be no clocks and I'll cry out
for heat not light.

This lady is stuck
on an elevator
shuddering
between the planets.

If life has passed this quickly,
a millennium is not all that long.
At fourteen
my sex fantasies
about Lucrezia Borgia:
I loved her name, the image
of her *rinascimento* undies,
her feet in the stirrups
of a golden saddle.
She's gone now
these many years.

Dad told me that we have time
so that everything won't happen at once.
For instance, deaths are spread out.
It would be real hard on people
if all the deaths for the year
occurred the same day.

Lemuribus vertebrates,
ossibus inter-tenebras —
"For the vertebrate ghosts,
for the bones among the darknesses,"
quoted the great Bringhurst,
who could have conquered Manhattan
and returned it to the natives,

who might have continued dancing
on the rocky sward.

The stillness
of dog shadows.

Here is time:
In the crotch of limbs
the cow's skull grew
into the tree
and birds nested in the mouth
year after year.

Human blood still fertilizes
the crops of Yurp.
The humus owns names:
Fred and Ted from old Missouri,
Cedric and Basil from Cornwall,
Heinz and Hans from Stuttgart,
Fyodor and Gretel in final embrace
beside raped Sylvie,
clod to clod.

The actual speed of life
is so much slower
we could have lived
exactly seven times as long
as we did.

These calendars
with pussy photos

send us a mixed message:
Marilyn Monroe stretched out
in unwingéd victory,
pink against red and reaching
not for the president or Nembutal
but because, like cats,
we like to do so.

Someday
like rockets without shells
we'll head for the stars.

On my newly devised calendar
there are only three days a month.
All the rest is space
so that night and day
don't feel uncomfortable
within my confines.
I'm not pushing them around,
making them do this and that.

Just this once
cows are shuffling over the hard rock
of the creek bed.
Two ravens in the black oak
purling whistles, coos, croaks,
raven-talk for the dead wild cow's
hindquarter in the grass,
the reddest of reds,
hips crushed when lassoed.
The cow dogs, blue heelers,

first in line for the meat,
all tugging like Africa.
Later, a stray sister
sniffs the femur bone,
bawls in boredom or lament.
In this sun's clock the bone
will become white, whiter, whitest.

The soul's decorum
dissembles
when she understands
that ashes have never
returned to wood.

Even running downstream
I couldn't step
into the same river once
let alone twice.

At first the sound
of the cat drinking water
was unendurable,
then it was broken by a fly
heading north,
a curve-billed thrasher
swallowing a red berry,
a dead sycamore leaf
suspended on its way to earth
by a breeze so slight
it went otherwise unnoticed.

The girl in the many-windowed bedroom
with full light coming in from the south
and the sun broken by trees,
has never died.

My friend's great-grandfather
lived from 1798 until 1901.

When a place is finished
you realize it went
like a truly beloved dog
whose vibrance had made
you think it would last forever;
becoming slightly sick,
then well and new again
though older, then sick
again, a long sickness.
A home burial.

They don't appear to have
firmed up their idea when time
started so we can go it alone.
"From birth to old age
it's just you," said Foyan.
So after T'ang foolery and Tancred
(the Black Pope of Umbanda)
I've lived my life in sevens,
not imagining that God could holler,
"Bring me my millennium!"
The sevens are married to each other
by what dogs I owned at the time,

where I fished and hunted,
appealing storms, solstice dinners,
loves and deaths, all the events
that are the marrow of the gods.

O lachrymae sonorense.
From the ground
paced the stars through the ribs
of ocotillo, thin and black
each o'clock till dawn,
rosy but no fingers except
these black thin stalks
directing a billion bright stars,
captured time swelling outward
for us if we are blessed
to be here on the ground,
night sky shot with measured stars,
night sky without end
amen.

NORTH

The mind of which we are unaware is aware of us.
— R.D. LAING

The rising sun not beet
or blood,
but sea–rose red.

I amplified my heartbeat
one thousand times;
the animals at first confused,
then decided I was another
thunder being.

While talking directly to god
my attention waxed and waned.
I have a lot on my mind.

I worked out
to make myself as strong
as water.

After all these years
of holding the world together
I let it roll down the hill
into the river.

One tree leads
to another,
walking on
this undescribed earth.

I have dreamed
myself back
to where
I already am.

On a cold day
bear, coyote, cranes.
On a rainy night
a wolf with yellow eyes.
On a windy day
eleven kestrels looking
down at me.
On a hot afternoon
the ravens floated over
where I sunk
myself in the river.

Way out there
in unknown country
I walked at night
to scare myself.

Who is this other,
the secret sharer,
who directs the hand
that twists the heart,
the voice calling out to me
between feather and stone
the hour before dawn?

Somehow
I have turned into
an old brown man
in a green coat.

Having fulfilled
my obligations
my heart moves lightly
to this downward dance.

BEAR

Bear died standing up,
paws on log,
howling. Shot
right through the heart.

The hunter only wanted the head,
the hide. I ate her
so she wouldn't go to waste,
dumped naked in a dump,
skinless, looking like ourselves
if we had been flayed,
red as death.

Now there are bear dreams
again for the bear-eater: O god,
the bears have come down the hill,
bears from everywhere on earth,
all colors, sizes, filtering
out of the woods behind the cabin.

A half-mile up
I plummeted toward the river to die,
pushed there. Then pinions creaked;
I flew downstream until I clutched
a white pine, the mind stepping back
to see half-bird, half-bear,
waking in the tree to wet
fur and feathers.

Hotei and bear
sitting side by side,

disappear into each other.
Who is to say
which of us is one?

We loaded the thousand-pound logs
by hand, the truck swaying.
Paused to caress my friend and helper,
the bear beside me, eye to eye,
breath breathing breath.

And now tonight, a big blue
November moon. Startled to find myself
wandering the edge of a foggy
tamarack marsh, scenting the cold
wet air, delicious in the moonglow.
Scratched against swart hemlock,
an itch to give it all up, shuffling
empty-bellied toward home, the yellow
square of cabin light between trees,
the human shape of yellow light,
to turn around,
to give up again this human shape.

TWILIGHT

For the first time
far in the distance
he could see his twilight
wrapping around the green hill
where three rivers start,
and sliding down toward him
through the trees until it reached
the blueberry marsh and stopped,
telling him to go away, not now,
not for the time being.

RETURN TO YESENIN

For only in praising is my heart still mine,
so violently do I know the world
— RAINER MARIA RILKE, *The Sonnets to Orpheus*

I forgot to say that at the moment of death Yesenin
stood there like a misty-eyed pioneer woman trying
to figure out what happened. Were the children
still in the burning barn with the bawling cows?
He was too sensitive for words, and the idea of a rope
was a wound he couldn't stop picking at. To step
back from this swinging man twisting clockwise
is to see how we mine ourselves too deeply,
that way down there we can break through the soul's
rock into a black underground river that sweeps us away.
To be frank, I'd rather live to feed my dogs,
knowing the world says *no* in ten thousand ways
and *yes* in only a few. The dogs don't need another
weeping Jesus on the cross of Art, strumming the scars
to keep them alive, tending them in a private
garden as if our night-blooming tumors were fruit.
I let you go for twenty years and am now only
checking if you're really dead. There was an urge
to put a few bullets through Nixon's coffin or a big,
sharp wooden stake, and a girl told me she just saw
Jimi Hendrix at an AIDS benefit in Santa Monica.
How could I disbelieve her when her nipples
were rosebuds, though you had to avoid the snakes
in her hair. If you had hung yourself in Argentina
you would have twisted counterclockwise. We can't
ask if it was worth it, can we? Anymore than we can
ask a whale its mother's name. Too bad we couldn't

go to Mexico together and croak a few small gods
back to life. I've entered my third act and am
still following my songs on that thin line between
woods and field, well short of the mouth of your hell.

SONORAN RADIO

(freely translated)

Looking at a big moon too long
rusts the eyes.

The raped girl stood all day naked
in the cold rain holding a plastic Virgin.
Their colors ran into the ground.

Tonight the Big Dipper poured down
its dark blood into the Sea of Cortez,
El Oso Grande, the hemorrhaged bear.

In the supermarket beef feet, chicken feet,
one lone octopus losing its charm.
An old woman named Octavia
who stared at my blind eye
carried out the 100 lb. gunnysack of pintos,
a bag of groceries in the other hand.

Just over the mountains
this other country, despised
and forsaken, makes more sense.
It admits people are complicated,
it tries to ignore its sufferings,
it cheats and loves itself,
it admits God might be made
of stone.

The red bird sits
on the dead brown snake.

The lobo admits its mistake
right after eating
the poisoned calf.

In the forms of death
we are all the same;
destinies are traded
at the very highest levels
in very high buildings
in clear view of the dump-pickers.

My heart and your heart!

The horses are running from flies.
Twenty-three horses run
around and around from the flies
in the big mesquite *retaque* corral
while five boys watch,
each one smaller
than the next biggest.

In the valley of the Toltecs
the American hunter from Palm Beach
shot one thousand white-winged doves
in a single day, all by himself.

The shark was nearly on shore
when it ate the child in three bites
and the mother kicked the shark in the eye.

The dopers killed the old doctor
in the mountain village,
but then the doctor's patients
stoned the dopers to death,
towing their bodies through town
behind Harley Davidsons.

It is the unpardonable music
stretching the soul
thinner than the skin.
Everyone knows they are not alone
as they suffer the music together
that gives them greater range
for greater suffering.

In the vision
the Virgin who sat in the sycamore
speaks in the voice
of the elegant trogon,
a bird so rare it goes
mateless for centuries.

The lagoon near the oil refinery
outside Tampico caught fire one night.
Everywhere tarpon were jumping
higher than a basketball hoop,
covered with oily flames,
the gill-plates rattling,
throwing off burning oil.

The black dove and white dove
intermarried, producing not brown doves,
but some white doves and black doves.
Down the line, however,
born in our garden a deep-yellow dove
more brilliant than gold
and blind as a bat.
She sits on my shoulder
cooing night songs in the day,
sleeping a few minutes at noon
and always at midnight, wakes
as if from a nightmare
screaming "Guadalupe!"

She said that outside Magdalena
on a mountainside
she counted thirteen guitarists
perched just below a cave
from which they tried to evoke
the usual flow
of blood and flowers.

Up in the borderland mountains
the moon fell slowly on Animas Peak
until it hit it directly
and broke like an egg,
spilling milk on the talus
and scree, sliding in a flood
through a dozen canyons.
The wind rose to fifty knots,

burning the moon
deep into the skin.

In a seaside restaurant
in Puerto Vallarta
a Bosnian woman killed a Serbian man
with a dinner fork,
her big arm pumping the tines
like a jackhammer
before the frightened diners
who decided not to believe it.
She escaped the police net,
fleeing into the green mountains,
fork in hand.

The praying mantis crawled
up the left nostril of our burro
and killed it.

Nightjars and goat suckers,
birds from the far edge of twilight
carrying ghosts from place to place –
Just hitching a ride, the ghosts
say to the birds, slapping
on the harness of black thread.
Even in *el norte* the whippoorwill's
nest is lined with the gossamer thread
of this ghost harness.

The cow dogs
tore apart

and ate
the pregnant housecat.

The gray hawk
(only twenty pair left in the U.S.)
flew close over
the vermillion flycatcher
perched on the tip
of the green juniper tree.

The waitress in the diner
where I ate my *menudo*
told me that Christ actually
bled to death. Back in those days
nails were the same as railroad spikes,
and the sun was hot as hell.
She sees the Resurrection
without irony or backspin.
"We are so lucky," she said.
"I couldn't live with all the things
I've done wrong in my life.
I feel better when I'm forgiven."

His dog sneezed
and crawled under a pickup
to get away from the sun.
The guitar and concertina music
swept down the mountainside
from the old cowboy's funeral,
hat and bridle
hanging from a white cross

in a cluster of admirable
plastic flowers.

The ravens are waiting
in the oak at twilight
for the coyotes to come
and open up the dead steer.
The ravens can't break through
cowhide with their beaks
and have been there since dawn
eager for the coyotes to get things started.
There's plenty for everyone.

These black beetles,
big as a thumb,
are locked in dead embrace
either in love or rage.

The bull does not want
to be caught. For five
hours and as many miles
on a hot morning
three cowboys and a half-dozen
cowdogs have worked
the bull toward the pen.
The truck is ready to take
him to the sale. He's known
as a baloney bull, inferring
his destiny: old, used up,
too lazy and tired to mount cows.
Meanwhile he's bawling, blowing

snot, charging, hooking a horn
at the horses, dogs, a stray tree.
Finally loaded, I said good-bye
to his blood-red eyes.
He rumbles, raises his huge neck
and bawls at the sun.

The cow dog licks her cancerous
and bloated teats.
Otherwise, she's the happiest
dog I know, always smiling,
always trying to help out.

I gave the woman seven roses
and she smiled, holding
the bouquet a couple of hours
at dusk before saying good-bye.
The next day I gave her
a brown calf and three chickens
and she took me to bed.
Over her shoulder a rose
petal fell for an hour.

From a thicket full
of red cardinals
burst seven black javelinas,
including three infants
the size of housecats.

There were so many birds
at the mountain spring

they drove one insane
at dawn and twilight;
bushes clotted with birds
like vulgar Christmas trees.
I counted thirteen hundred
of a hundred different kinds,
all frozen in place
when the gray hawk flew by,
its keening voice
the precise weight of death.

Magdalena kept taking off her clothes
for hours until there was nothing left,
not even a trace of moisture on the leather chair.
Perhaps it was because
she was a government employee
and had lost a child.
It was the sleight of her hand.
I never saw her again.

Another bowl of *menudo*
and she's on a rampage in a black
Guadalupe T-shirt: "We can't keep
working through the used part every day.
Everyone is tired of dope. Day in, day out,
the newspapers are full of dope news,
people are shot dead and not-so-dead,
sent to prison, and both police and criminals
are so bored with dope they weep
day and night, going about their jobs,

living and dying from this stupid dope.
There has to be more than dope. Understand?"

I dreamed here
before I arrived.
Chuck and whir
of elf owls above firelight,
dozens in the black oak
staring down into the fire
beyond which a thousand white sycamore
limbs move their legs into the night.
Sonoran moon gets red
again as she sets in the dust
we've colored with blood.

PREVIOUSLY
UNCOLLECTED
POEMS

1976–1990

HELLO WALLS

to Willie Nelson

How heavy I am. My feet sink into the ground and my knees
are rubbery, my head and brain propped with aluminum braces.
Life is short! I'm sinking through it at the speed of sound.
A feather is dropping with me in the vacuum. At bottom we'll
prove nothing except the fall is over for both of us. No matter
that I am richer than Satanta the Kiowa chief if you subtract
those millions of verdant acres which we did. In the prison
hospital he hurls himself headfirst from the third-story window.
Who wants to die like a white Christian? Even his animal skins
forgave him. But this has nothing to do with me – out the window
I can't see the army approach with cocked howitzers. There's
nothing but snow. How to lift myself out of this Egypt, wriggle
free, fly out of the page, out of the human condition like
a miraculous crow, like Satanta from the window, like birds
beneath the buffalo feet, griffins to a nest at the cathedral's
top. *Fly, fly away* the old song goes, climb a single note
and follow it, crazed mariachi, a shot tomcat, or Huxley
near death from cancer drops ten thousand hits of acid to go out
on a truly stupendous note, far above King David's zither,
the shriek of our space probe hitting Venus plum in the middle.

– from *Aisling,* summer 1976

411

SCRUBBING THE FLOOR
THE NIGHT A GREAT LADY DIED

Ruffian 1972–1975

Sunday, with two weeks of heat lifting from us in a light rain. A good day for work with the break in weather; then the race, the great horse faltering, my wife and daughter leaving the room in tears, the dinner strangely silent, with a dull, metallic yellow cast to the evening sun. We turn from the *repeats,* once is so much more than enough. So the event fades and late in the night writing in the kitchen I look at the floor soiled by the Airedales in the heatwave, tracking in the brackish dirt from the algae-covered pond. I want the grace of this physical gesture, filling the pail, scrubbing the floor after midnight, sweet country music from the radio and a drink or two; then the grotesque news bringing me up from the amnesia of the floor. How could a creature of such beauty merely disappear? I saw her as surely as at twilight I watched our own horses graze in the pasture. How could she wake so frantic, as if from a terrible dream? Then to continue with my scrubbing, saying it's only a horse but knowing that if I cannot care about a horse, I cannot care about earth herself. For she was so surely of earth, in earth; once so animate, sprung in some final, perfect form, running, running, saying, *"Look at me, look at me, what could be more wonderful than the way I move, tell me if there's something more wonderful, I'm the same as a great whale sounding."* But then who am I sunk on the floor scrubbing at this bitterness? It doesn't matter. A great creature died who took her body as far as bodies go toward perfection and I wonder how like Crazy Horse she seems to leave us so far behind.

– from *Natural World,* 1982

THE SAME GOOSE MOON

Peach sky
at sunset,
then (for a god's sake)
one leaf whirled
across the face
of the big October moon.

– from Book for Sensei, 1990

NEW POEMS

1998

GEO–BESTIARY

I

I can hear the cow dogs sleeping
in the dust, the windmill's
creak above thirty-three
sets of shrill mating birds.
The vultures fly above the corrals
so softly the air ignores them.
In all of the eons, past and future,
not one day clones itself.

2

I walked the same circular path today
in the creek bottom three times.
The first: a blur, roar of snowmelt
in creek, brain jumbling like the rolling
of river stones I watched carefully
with swim goggles long ago, hearing
the stones clack, click, and slow shuffle
along the gravel.
The second time: the creek is muddy,
a Mexican jay follows me at a polite
distance, the mind slows to the color
of wet, beige grass, a large raindrop
hits the bridge of my nose, the remote
mountain canyon has a fresh dusting
of snow. My head hurts pleasantly.
The third time: my life depends
on the three million two hundred seventy-seven
thousand three hundred and thirty-three
pebbles locked into the ground so I
don't fall through the thin skin of earth
on which there is a large coyote-turd full
of Manzanita berries I stepped over twice
without noticing it, a piece of ancient chert,
a fragment of snakeskin, an owl eye
staring from a hole in an Emory oak,
the filaments of eternity hanging in the earthly
air like the frailest of beacons seen
from a ship mortally far out in the sea.

3

That dew-wet glistening wild iris
doesn't know where it comes from,
what drove the green fuse, the poet said,
up and out into the flowering I see
in the dank flat of the creek, my eye
drawn there by a Virginia rail who keeps
disappearing as they do, unlike the flower
which stays exactly in the place the heron stands
every day, the flower no doubt fertilized
by heron shit, or deeper – those rocky bones
my daughter found of the Jurassic lizard.
I said to the flower one brain-bleeding morning
that I don't know where I came from either
or where I'm going, such a banal statement
however true. O wild iris here today and soon gone,
the earth accepts us both without comment.

4

Some eco-ninny released
at least a hundred tame white doves
at our creek crossing. What a feast
he innocently offered, coyotes in the yard
for the first time, a pair of great horned
owls, male and then the female
ululating, two ferruginous hawks,
and then at dawn today all song-
birds vamoosed at a startling shadow,
a merlin perched in the willow,
ur-falcon, bird-god, sweetly vengeful,
the white feathers of its meal,
a clump, among others, of red-spotted snow.

5

The little bull calf gets his soft pink
nuts clipped off, then is released
in a state of bafflement, wandering
this way and that, perhaps feeling
a tad lighter, an actual lacuna.
But like the rest of the culture these creatures
are quick healers, have been dumbed down
so far from their wild state they think we're harmless.
In the old days sometimes longhorns,
like the Lakota had, had the sense to attack
Cavalry contingents, goring what could be gored.
Even now a few, not quite bred or beaten
into senescence, struggle wildly with these invisible
telemetric collars wrapped tightly around our necks
though it's fatally illegal to take them off.

6

O BLM, BLM, and NFS,
what has your mother, the earth,
done to you that you rape and scalp
her so savagely, this beautiful woman
now mostly scar tissue?

7

O that girl, only young men
dare to look at her directly
while I manage the most sidelong of glances:
olive-skinned with a Modigliani throat,
lustrous obsidian hair, the narrowest
of waists and high French bottom, ample
breasts she tries to hide in a loose blouse.
Though Latino her profile is from a Babylonian
frieze and when she walks her small white dog
with brown spots she fairly floats along,
looking neither left nor right, meeting no one's
glance as if beauty was a curse. In the grocery
store when I drew close her scent was jacaranda,
the tropical flower that makes no excuses.
This geezer's heart swells stupidly to the dampish
promise. I walk too often in the cold shadow
of the mountain wall up the arroyo behind the house.
Empty pages are dry ice, numbing the hands and heart.
If I weep I do so in the shower so that no one,
not even I, can tell. To see her is to feel
time's cold machete against my grizzled neck,
puzzled that again beauty has found her home in threat.

8

Many a sharp-eyed pilot has noticed
while flying in late October
that remnant hummingbirds rob piggyback
rides on the backs of southward-flying geese.

9

I hedge when I say "my farm."
We don't ever own, we barely rent this earth.
I've even watched a boulder age,
changing the texture of its mosses
and cracking from cold back in 1983.
Squinting, it becomes a mountain fissure.
I've sat on this rock so long we celebrate
together our age, our mute geologic destiny.

10

I know a private mountain range with a big bowl in its center that you find by following the narrowest creek bed, sometimes crawling until you struggle through a thicket until you reach two large cupped hands of stone in the middle of which is a hill, a promontory, which would be called a mountain back home. There is iron in this hill and it sucks down summer lightning, thousands and thousands of strokes through time, shattering the gigantic top into a field of undramatic crystals that would bring a buck a piece at a rock show. I was here in a dark time and stood there and said, "I have put my poem in order on the threshold of my tongue," quoting someone from long, long ago, then got the hell off the mountain due to tremors of undetermined source. Later that night sleeping under an oak a swarm of elf owls (*Micrathene whitneyi*) descended to a half-dozen feet above my head and a thousand white sycamores undulated in the full moon, obviously the living souls of lightning strokes upside down along the arroyo bed. A modern man, I do not make undue connections though my heart wrenches daily against the unknowable, almighty throb and heave of the universe against my skin that sings a song for which we haven't quite found the words.

I I

Today the warblers undulate
fishlike, floating down,
lifting up with wing beats
while below me in the creek
minnows undulate birdlike,
floating down, lifting up with fin beats.
For a minute I lose the sense
of up and down.

12

I was hoping to travel the world
backward in my red wagon,
one knee in, the other foot pushing.
I was going to see the sights I'd imagined:
Spanish buildings, trellised with flowers,
a thousand Rapunzels brushing their long
black hair with street vendors singing
the lyrics of Lorca. I'd be towed
by a stray Miura over the green Pyrenees,
turning the bull loose before French customs.
At the edge of the forest René Char was roasting
a leg of lamb over a wood fire. We shared
a gallon of wine while mignonettes frolicked for us.
This all occurred to me forty-two
years ago while hoeing corn and it's time
for it all to come to pass along with my canoe
trip through Paris, with Jean Moreau trailing
a hand in the crystalline Seine, reading me Robert Desnos.
Why shouldn't this happen? I have to rid
myself of this last land mine, the unlived life.

13

Try as you might there's nothing
you can do about bird shadows
except try to head them off
and abruptly stop, letting them pass
by in peace. Looking up and down
at the very same moment is difficult
for a single-eyed man.
The ones coming behind you,
often cautious crows or ravens,
strike hard against the back and nape nerve.
Like most of life your wariness
is useless. You wobble
slightly dumbstruck, queasy,
then watch the shadow flit across
the brown wind-tormented grass.

14

As a geezer one grows tired of the story
of Sisyphus. Let that boulder stay
where it is and, by its presence,
exactly where it wished to be,
but then I'm old enough to have
forgotten what the boulder stood for?
I think of all of the tons of junk
the climbers have left up on Everest,
including a few bodies. Even the pyramids,
those imitation mountains, say to the gods,
"We can do it too." Despite planes
you can't get off the earth for long.
Even the dead meat strays behind, changing
shape, the words drift into the twilight
across the lake. I'm not bold enough
to give a poetry reading while alone
far out in the desert to a gathering
of saguaro and organ-pipe cactus
or listen to my strophes reverberate off a mountain
wall. At dawn I sat on a huge boulder
near Cave Creek deep in the Chiracahuas
and listened to it infer that it didn't want
to go way back up the mountain but liked
it near the creek where gravity bought
its passage so long ago. Everest told me
to get this crap off my head or stay at home
and make your own little pyramids.

15

Concha is perhaps seven. No one knows this cow dog's age for sure but of course she could care less. Let us weep for the grandeur of rebellious women. After a lifetime of service as a faithful tender of cattle her mind has changed itself. She's become daffy and won't do her job. She's the alpha bitch and leads the other cow dogs off on nightly runs after javelina and deer, maybe herding steers when she shouldn't, driving horses mad. They return worthlessly exhausted. Now the death sentence hangs above her mottled gray head like a halo of flies. She's chained to a mesquite, barking for hours without pause. I bring her biscuits on frosty mornings and she shivers without in her solitary confinement but inside it's obvious that she's hot and singing. Her head with its streaks of barbed-wire scars awaits the trigger finger. But then on a dark, wet morning, the grace of El Niño in this parched land, her reprieve arrives. She's being exiled to a ranch in Mexico just south of here where they need a crazed bitch who's kick-ass with range bulls. She'll drive one into an outhouse if that's what you want. This is a triumph beyond good-byes and I watch through the window as she leaves the barnyard in the back of a pickup, the wind and rain in her face, baring her teeth in anger or a smile, her uncertain future, which by nature she ignores, so much better to me than none.

16

My favorite stump straddles a gully a dozen
miles from any human habitation.
My eschatology includes scats, animal poop,
scatology so that when I nestle under this stump
out of the rain I see the scats of bear, bobcat,
coyote. I won't say that I feel at home
under this vast white pine stump, the roots
spread around me, so large in places no arms
can encircle them, as if you were under the body
of a mythic spider, the thunder ratcheting
the sky so that the earth hums beneath you.
Here is a place to think about nothing,
which is what I do. If the rain beats down
hard enough tiny creeks form beside my shit-strewn
pile of sand. The coyote has been eating mice,
the bear berries, the bobcat a rabbit. It's dry
enough so it doesn't smell except for ancient
wet wood and gravel, pine pitch, needles. Luckily
a sandhill crane nests nearby so that in June
if I doze I'm awakened by her cracked
and prehistoric cry, waking startled, feeling
the two million years I actually am.

17

I was sent far from my land of bears.
It wasn't an asylum but a resting place
to get well buttoned-up against my fugal state
wherein whirl is both the king and queen,
the brain-gods who stir a thousand revolutions
a second the contents of this graying cocotte.
Stop it please. Please stop it please.
There was one other poet from Yankeeland
who rubbed himself, including private parts,
with sandpaper. His doctor searched his room,
even his anus where he had secreted a tightly
bound roll. Across the wide yard and women's
quarters a lovely soprano sang TV jingles.
One day it was, "Fly the friendly skies of United,"
over and over. Her friend fed her peanut butter
and marshmallows to quell her voice, plus
a daily goblet of Thorazine. If you dive down deep
enough there are no words to bring you up. Not my
problem. If you fly too high there are no words
to help you land. I went back to my land of bears
and learned to bob like an apple on the river's surface.

18

I was commanded, in a dream naturally,
to begin the epitaphs of thirty-three friends
without using grand words like love pity pride
sacrifice doom honor heaven hell earth:

1. O you deliquescent flower
2. O you always loved long naps
3. O you road-kill Georgia possum
4. O you broken red lightbulb
5. O you mosquito smudge fire
6. O you pitiless girl missing a toe
7. O you big fellow in pale-blue shoes
8. O you poet without a book
9. O you lichen without tree or stone
10. O you lion without a throat
11. O you homeless scholar with dirty feet
12. O you jungle bird without a jungle
13. O you city with a single street
14. O you tiny sun without an earth
15. Forgive me for saying good-night quietly
16. Forgive me for never answering the phone
17. Forgive me for sending too much money
18. Pardon me for fishing during your funeral
19. Forgive me for thinking of your lovely ass
20. Pardon me for burning your last book
21. Forgive me for making love to your widow
22. Pardon me for never mentioning you
23. Forgive me for not knowing where you're buried
24. O you forgotten famous person
25. O you great singer of banal songs
26. O you shrike in the darkest thicket

27. O you river with too many dams
28. O you orphaned vulture with no meat
29. O you who sucked a shotgun to orgasm
30. Forgive me for raising your ghost so often
31. Forgive me for naming a bird after you
32. Forgive me for keeping a nude photo of you
33. We'll all see God but not with our eyes

19

I sat on a log fallen over a river and heard
that like people each stretch had a different voice
varying with the current, the nature
of its bed and banks, logjams, boulders,
alder or cedar branches, low-slung
and sweeping the current, the hush of eddies.
In a deep pool I saw the traces of last night's moon.

20

Who is it up to if it isn't up to you?
In motels I discover how ugly I am,
the mirrors at home too habitual to be noted.
I chose methodically to be anti-beautiful,
Christian fat keeps you safe from adultery!
With delight I drown my lungs in smoke
and drink that extra bottle of wine
that brings me so much closer to the gods.
Up the road a dozen wetbacks were caught
because one stopped at a ranch house, desperate
for a cigarette. Olive oil and pork sausage
are pratfalls, an open secret to the stove.
In the newspaper I read that thirty-two
dairy cows ate themselves to death on grain
by shaking loose an automatic feeder
("They just don't know any better," the vet said).
Of course false modesty is a family habit.
The zone-tailed hawk looks like and mimics
the harmless turkey vultures with which it often
flies for concealment, stoops in flight and devours
the creatures who thought, "It's just a vulture."

21

In the Cabeza Prieta from a hillock I saw no human sign for a thousand square miles except for a stray intestinal vapor trail with which we mar the sky. I naturally said, "I'm alone." The immense ocotillo before me is a thousand-foot-high rope to heaven but then you can't climb its spiny branches. In Daniel's Wash I heard and saw the great mother of crotalids, a rattler, and at a distance her rattles sounded exactly like Carmen Miranda's castanets, but closer, a string of firecrackers. In 1957 in New York I was with Anne Frank who was trying to be a writer but they wouldn't buy her dark stories. We lived on Macdougal south of Houston and I worked as a sandhog digging tunnels until I was crushed to death. She cooked fairly well (flanken, chicken livers, herring salad). Now Ed Abbey rides down from the Growler Mountains on a huge mountain ram, bareback and speechless. This place is a fearsome goddess I've met seven times in a decade. She deranges my mind with the strangest of beauties, her Venusian flora mad to puncture the skin. It's ninety degrees and I wonder if I'm walking so far within her because I wish to die, so parched I blow dust from my throat. Finally I reach the hot water in my car and weep at the puny sight. Is this what I've offered this wild beauty? Literally a goddamned car, a glittering metallic tumor.

22

"Life's too short to be a whore anymore,"
I sang out to the Atlantic Ocean
from my seaside room in St. Malo,
the brain quite fugal until I took
a long walk seaward at low tide
and watched closely old French ladies
gathering crustaceans. When they left
they shook their fingers saying, "*marée, marée,*"
and I watched them walk away toward shore
where I had no desire to go. A few
stopped and waved their arms wildly.
The tide! The tide goes out, then comes in
in this place huge, twenty feet or so,
the tidal bore sweeping slowly in
but faster than me. I still didn't want to leave
because I was feeling like a very old whore
who wanted to drown, but then this wispy
ego's pulse drifted away with a shitting gull.
Before I died I must eat the three-leveled
"plateau" of these crustaceans with two bottles
of Sancerre. It's dinner that drives the beaten
dog homeward, tail half-up, half-down,
no dog whore but trotting legs, an empty stomach.

23

My soul grew weak and polluted during captivity, a zoo creature, frantic but most often senescent. One day in the Upper Peninsula I bought a painting at a yard sale of the supposed interior of a clock. The tag said, "Real Oil Painting Nineteen Bucks." People around me grinned, knowing I wasn't a yard-sale pro. Never go to a supermarket when you're hungry, my mother said, or a yard sale after a Côtes du Rhône. The painting was quite dark as there's little sunlight within clocks but the owners had wiped it with oil and there was a burnished glow to its burnt sienna. I couldn't see into the cavern in the center but I didn't have my glasses with me. Back at the cabin I was lucky enough to have the magnifying glass that comes with the *Compact Oxford English Dictionary,* the true source of agony. There were grinning mice sailing along on Eilshemius-type clouds in a corner of the clock's metallic shell, and miniature assemblage print that said, "flyways, byways, highways" in a lighter cavern, also "Je souffre but so what," also "I am a buggered cherubim," an alarming statement. On the central cavern walls there were the usual cogs and wheels, straightforward, not melting Dali-esques. In the lower left-hand corner it was signed "Felicia" with a feminine bottom from which emerged a candle, lighting the artist's name. Here was a wedding present for a couple you didn't really like. Children, even future artists, should never take the backs off of discarded Big Bens. They'll never make sense of these glum, interior stars with their ceaseless ticking, saying that first you're here and then you're not.

24

A whiff of that dead bird along the trail
is a whiff of what I'd smell like
if I was lucky enough to die
well back in the woods or out in the desert.
The heavy Marine compass doesn't remind
me that I'm somewhere in America,
likely in northern Michigan by the maple and alder,
the wildly blooming sugarplum and dogwood,
wandering aimlessly in great circles
as your gait tends to pull you slowly aside,
my one leg slightly distorted at birth
though I was fifty before my mother told me,
but then from birth we're all mortally wounded.
When I was a stray dog in New York City
in 1957, trying to eat on a buck a day
while walking thousands of blocks
in that human forest I thought was enchanted,
not wanting to miss anything but missing
everything because at nineteen dreams
daily burst the brain, dismay the senses,
the interior weeping drowning your steps,
your mind an underground river
running counter to your tentative life.
"Our body is a molded river," said wise Novalis.
Bloody brain and heart, also mind and soul finally
becoming a single river, flowing in a great circle,
flowing from darkness to blessed darkness,
still wondering above all else what kind of beast am I?

25

The resplendent female "elegant trogon,"
her actual name, appeared at my study
window the very moment my heroine died
(in a novel of course) so that my hair
bristled like the time a lion coughed right
outside our thin screen-walled shack.
What does this mean? Nothing whatsoever,
except itself, I am too quick to answer.
This bird is so rare she never saw it.
I had expected her soul to explode
into a billion raindrops, falling on the farm
where she was born, or far out in the ocean
where she drowned, precisely where I once saw
two giant sea turtles making love.
Full fathom five thy lovely sister lies,
tumbling north in the Gulfstream current,
but then the soul rose up as vapor, blown west-
ward to the Sea of Cortez, up a canyon, inhabiting
this quetzal bird who chose to appear at my window.
This all took three seconds by my geologic watch.

26

In Montana the badger looks at me in fear
and buries himself where he stood
in the soft sandy gravel
only moments ago. I have to think
it's almost like our own deaths
assuming we had the wit to save money
by digging our own graves or gathering
the wood for the funeral pyre.
But then the badger does it to stay alive, carrying
his thicket, his secret room in his powerful claws.

27

She said in LA of course that she'd be reincarnated as an Indian princess, and I tried to recall any Lakota or Anishinabe princesses. I said how about wheat berries, flakes of granite on a mountainside, a green leaf beginning to dry out on the ground, a microbe within a dog turd, the windfall apple no one finds, an ordinary hawk fledgling hitting a high-tension wire, apricot blossoms from that old fallow tree? Less can be more she agreed. It might be nice to try something else, say a tree that only gets to dance if the wind comes up but I refuse to believe this lettuce might be Grandma – more likely the steak that they don't serve here. We go from flesh to flesh, she thought, with her nose ring and tongue tack, inscrutable to me but doubtless genetic. There is no lesser flesh whether it grows feathers or fur, scales or hairy skin. The coyote wishes to climb the moonbeam she cannot be, the wounded raven to stay in the cloud forever. Whatever we are we don't quite know it, waiting for a single thought as lovely as April's sycamore.

28

The wallet is as big as earth
and we snuffle, snorkel, lip lap
at money's rankest genitals,
buried there as money gophers, money worms,
hibernate our lives away with heads
well up money's asshole, eating, drinking,
sleeping there in money's shitty dark.
That's money, folks, the perverse love
thereof, as if we swam carrying an anchor
or the blinders my grandpa's horses wore
so that while ploughing they wouldn't notice
anything but the furrow ahead, not certainly
the infinitely circular horizon of earth.
Not the money for food and bed but the endless
brown beyond that. I'm even saving
up for my past, by god, healing the twelve-hour
days in the fields or laying actual concrete blocks.
The present passes too quickly to notice
and I've never had a grip on the future,
even as an idea. As a Pleistocene dunce
I want my wife and children to be safe
in the past, and then I'll look up from my money-
fucking grubbing work to watch the evening
shadows fleeing across the green field next door,
tethered to these shadows dragging toward night.

29

How can I be alone when these brain cells
chat to me their million messages
a minute. But sitting there in the ordinary
trance that is any mammal's birthright, say on a desert
boulder or northern stump, a riverbank,
we can imitate a barrel cactus, a hemlock tree,
the water that flows through time as surely
as ourselves. The mind loses its distant
machine-gun patter, becomes a frog's
occasional croak. A trout's last jump in the dark,
a horned owl's occasional hoot,
or in the desert alone at night
the voiceless stars light my primate
fingers that I lift up to curl
around their bright cosmic bodies.

30

How much better these actual dreams
than the vulgar "hoped for," the future's
golden steps which are really old
cement blocks stacked at a door that can
never open because we
are already inside.
Is all prayer just barely short of the lip
of whining as if, however things are,
they can't possibly be quite right
(what I don't have I probably should),
the sole conviction praying for sick children?
But true dreams arrived without being
summoned, incomprehensibly old and without
your consent: the animal that is running
is you under the wide gray sky, the sound
of those banal drumbeats is the heart's true reflection,
all water over your head is bottomless,
the sky above we've learned quite without limits.
Running, he wears the skins of animals
to protect his ass in the misery of running,
stopping at the edge of the green earth
without the fulsome courage to jump off.
He builds a hut there and makes the music
he's never heard except in the pulse of dreams.

31

A few long miles up Hog Canyon
this rare late-March heat is drawing forth
the crotalids from their homes of earth and rock
where they had sensed me scrambling over them
while hunting quail. It is the dread
greenish brown Mojave I fear the most,
known locally as "dog killer," lifting
its wary head higher than you think possible,
coiling its length beneath itself
as if a boxer could carry a single, fatal punch.
This is the farthest reach from the petting zoo
like my Africa's dream black mamba.
I tell her I'm sorry I shot a cousin rattler
in our bedroom. How idiotic. She's a cocked
.357 snake, rattling "Get the hell out of here.
This land is my land when I awake.
Walk here in the cool of morning or not at all."
She's my childhood myth of the kiss of death
and I'm amazed how deftly I fling myself backward
down a long steep hill, my setter Rose frightened
by my unconscious, verbless bellows. Perhaps
if I'm dying from some painful disease
I'll catch and hold you like Cleopatra's asp
to my breast, a truly inventive suicide.

32

How the love of Tarzan in Africa haunted my childhood, strapped with this vivid love of an imaginary wild, the white orphan as king of nature with all creatures at his beck and call, monkey talk, Simba! Kreegah! Gomanganini! The mysterious Jane was in his tree house in leather loincloth and bra before one had quite figured out why she should be there. Perhaps this was all only a frantic myth to allay our fear of the darkest continent and help us defeat a world that will never be ours after we had tried so hard to dispose of our own indians. The blacks were generally grand if not influenced too much by an evil witch doctor, or deceived by venal white men, often German or French, while a current Tarzan, far from the great Johnny Weismuller, has the body builder's more than ample tits, tiny waist and blow-dried hair, Navajo booties somehow, while the newest Jane has a Dutch accent and runs through a Mexican forest (if you know flora) in shorts and cowboy boots screaming in absolute alarm at nearly everything though she simply passed out when a black tied her rather attractively way up in a tree. What can we make of this Aryan myth gone truly bad, much worse than Sambo's tigers turning to butter for his pancakes, much more decrepit than noble Robin Hood; or how we made our landscape safe for mega-agriculture and outdoor cow factories by shooting all the buffalo, and red kids fast asleep in tents at Sand Creek and elsewhere, the Church climbing to heaven on the backs of Jews; or that we could destroy the Yellow Plague in Vietnam? The girl or boy with their brown dog in the woods on Sunday afternoon must learn first to hold their noses at requests to march. But Tarzan swinging over the whole world on his convenient vines, knows that bugs, snakes, beasts and birds, are of the angelic orders, safe forever from men and their thundersticks and rancid clothes, and Jane's lambent butt and English accent singing him to sleep in their treetop home, she waving down at the profuse eyelashes of a sleeping elephant.

33

Coyote's bloody face makes me
wonder what he ate, also reminds
me of when I sliced my hand
sharpening the scythe to cut weeds.
What the hell is this blood we mostly see
on TV, movies, the doctor's office, hospitals?
The first two remote and dishonest,
the second two less so but readily expunged,
but not the massive dark-red pool beneath
the shrimper's neck in 1970, his trachea
a still-pulsing calamari ring.
I don't care how many quarts of this red
juice I'm carrying around as it flows
through its pitch-dark creeks and rivers.
We must learn to rock our own cradles.
I don't want to get ahead or behind myself
fueled by this red gasoline, legs stretching
as if eager to pass over the edge of earth
or trotting backward into the inglorious past.
Tonight its pump is thumping as when an airplane's
engine stutters, thinking too much of those I loved
who died long ago, the girl sitting in the apple
tree, the red sun sinking beneath her feet,
how god plucked her off earth with his careless
tweezers because she plucked a flower with her toes.

34

Not how many different birds I've seen
but how many have seen me,
letting the event go unremarked
except for the quietest sense of malevolence,
dead quiet, then restarting their lives
after fear, not with song, which is reserved
for lovers, but the harsh and quizzical
chatter with which we all get by:
but if she or he passes by and the need
is felt we hear the music that transcends all fear,
and sometimes the simpler songs that greet sunrise,
rain or twilight. Here I am.
They sing what and where they are.

INDEX OF TITLES

INDEX OF FIRST LINES

458

461

ABOUT THE AUTHOR

Jim Harrison is the author of twenty books, numerous screenplays, and served for several years as the food columnist for *Esquire* magazine. His work has been translated into twenty-two languages and produced as four feature-length films. As a young poet he co-edited *Sumac* magazine and earned a National Endowment for the Arts grant and a Guggenheim Fellowship. Mr. Harrison divides his time between northern Michigan and southern Arizona.

BOOKS BY JIM HARRISON

Poetry

Plain Song

Locations

Outlyer & Ghazals

Letters to Yesenin

Returning to Earth

Selected & New Poems

The Theory & Practice of Rivers

After Ikkyū

Nonfiction

Just Before Dark

Novels

Wolf

A Good Day to Die

Farmer

Warlock

Sundog

Dalva

The Road Home

Novella Trilogies

Legends of the Fall

The Woman Lit by Fireflies

Julip

• • •

This book was designed and composed in the typeface Bembo
by Valerie Brewster, Scribe Typography. In 1929, Monotype
attempted to capture the spirit of type engraved on steel punches
and cast in metal in the early Renaissance. They used a travelogue
written by Pietro Bembo and set by Francesco Griffo as their
inspiration. Griffo's lively refinements to the roman letter
give Bembo beauty and legibility. Printed on archival
quality 55# Perfection Antique Recycled at
Maple-Vail Book Manufacturing.

The Shape of the Journey is also issued in a signed, limited
.   edition of two hundred fifty copies bound in
Japanese cloth and paper over boards, and slipcased
by the Campbell-Logan Bindery. An additional
twenty-six copies have been lettered
A to Z, and are *hors commerce*.